Agricultural Economics and Agri-Food Business

Edited by Orhan Özçatalbaş

Published in London, United Kingdom

Agricultural Economics and Agri-Food Business
http://dx.doi.org/10.5772/intechopen.107821
Edited by Orhan Özçatalbaş

Contributors
Abdul Halik, Agung Hendriadi, Agus Budiyanto, Agustinus N. Kairupan, Akhmad Junaidi, Alvi Yani, Amos Lukas, Amsal Rasyid, Arief Arianto, August Polakitan, Bonnie O. Benyamin, Bukola Margaret Popoola, Comfort Tosin Olateru, Derek Polakitan, Eko Bhakti Susetyo, Ermi E. Koeslulat, Evgeniya Borysevych, Gabriel H. Joseph, Guntur Haryanto, Henky Henanto, Heri Wahyudianto, Heryoki Yohanes, Himawan Adinegoro, Huda M. Elmatsani, Iraj Malek Mohammadi, Jamal Farajollah Hoseini, Joko Saptohadi, Josep Ginting, Kusumawati Dewi Budiarti, Lamhot Parulian Manalu, Lanjar Sumarno, Meivie Lintang, Mochammad Yusuf Djafar, Mulyana Hadipernata, Nasruddin, Neda Seyedan, Nenie Yustiningsih, Noverina Sjafrina, Olga Zamlynska, Olusolabomi Jose Adefioye, Payung Layuk, Pooja Mehra, Puji Astuti, Reza Moghaddasi, Rienoviar, Roosganda Elizabeth, S.Joni Munarso, Sahlan, Sari Intan Kailaku, Simran Ahuja, Sitti Ramlah, Subandrio Subandrio, Suharto Ngudiwaluyo, Taufik Hidayat, Tetyana Shabatura, Viktor Zamlynskyi, Wahyu Purwanto

First published in London, United Kingdom, 2024 by IntechOpen
IntechOpen is the global imprint of INTECHOPEN LIMITED, registered in England and Wales, registration number: 11086078, 167-169 Great Portland Street, London, W1W 5PF, United Kingdom

British Library Cataloguing-in-Publication Data
A catalogue record for this book is available from the British Library

Additional hard and PDF copies can be obtained from orders@intechopen.com

Agricultural Economics and Agri-Food Business
Edited by Orhan Özçatalbaş
p. cm.

This title is part of the Sustainable Development Book Series, Volume 16
Topic: Sustainable Economy and Fair Society
Series Editor: Usha Iyer-Raniga
Topic Editor: Antonella Petrillo

Print ISBN 978-1-80356-650-4
Online ISBN 978-1-80356-651-1
eBook (PDF) ISBN 978-1-80356-652-8
ISSN 2753-6580

For EU product safety concerns:
IN TECH d.o.o., Prolaz Marije Krucifikse Kozulić 3, 51000 Rijeka, Croatia,
info@intechopen.com or visit our website at intechopen.com.

IntechOpen Book Series
Sustainable Development
Volume 16

Aims and Scope of the Series

Transforming our World: the 2030 Agenda for Sustainable Development endorsed by United Nations and 193 Member States, came into effect on Jan 1, 2016, to guide decision making and actions to the year 2030 and beyond. Central to this Agenda are 17 Goals, 169 associated targets and over 230 indicators that are reviewed annually. The vision envisaged in the implementation of the SDGs is centered on the five Ps: People, Planet, Prosperity, Peace and Partnership. This call for renewed focused efforts ensure we have a safe and healthy planet for current and future generations.

This Series focuses on covering research and applied research involving the five Ps through the following topics:

1. Sustainable Economy and Fair Society that relates to SDG 1 on No Poverty, SDG 2 on Zero Hunger, SDG 8 on Decent Work and Economic Growth, SDG 10 on Reduced Inequalities, SDG 12 on Responsible Consumption and Production, and SDG 17 Partnership for the Goals

2. Health and Wellbeing focusing on SDG 3 on Good Health and Wellbeing and SDG 6 on Clean Water and Sanitation

3. Inclusivity and Social Equality involving SDG 4 on Quality Education, SDG 5 on Gender Equality, and SDG 16 on Peace, Justice and Strong Institutions

4. Climate Change and Environmental Sustainability comprising SDG 13 on Climate Action, SDG 14 on Life Below Water, and SDG 15 on Life on Land

5. Urban Planning and Environmental Management embracing SDG 7 on Affordable Clean Energy, SDG 9 on Industry, Innovation and Infrastructure, and SDG 11 on Sustainable Cities and Communities.

The series also seeks to support the use of cross cutting SDGs, as many of the goals listed above, targets and indicators are all interconnected to impact our lives and the decisions we make on a daily basis, making them impossible to tie to a single topic.

Meet the Series Editor

Usha Iyer-Raniga is a professor in the School of Property and Construction Management at RMIT University. Usha co-leads the One Planet Network's Sustainable Buildings and Construction Programme (SBC), a United Nations 10 Year Framework of Programmes on Sustainable Consumption and Production (UN 10FYP SCP) aligned with Sustainable Development Goal 12. The work also directly impacts SDG 11 on Sustainable Cities and Communities. She completed her undergraduate degree as an architect before obtaining her Masters degree from Canada and her Doctorate in Australia. Usha has been a keynote speaker as well as an invited speaker at national and international conferences, seminars and workshops. Her teaching experience includes teaching in Asian countries. She has advised Austrade, APEC, national, state and local governments. She serves as a reviewer and a member of the scientific committee for national and international refereed journals and refereed conferences. She is on the editorial board for refereed journals and has worked on Special Issues. Usha has served and continues to serve on the Boards of several not-for-profit organisations and she has also served as panel judge for a number of awards including the Premiers Sustainability Award in Victoria and the International Green Gown Awards. Usha has published over 100 publications, including research and consulting reports. Her publications cover a wide range of scientific and technical research publications that include edited books, book chapters, refereed journals, refereed conference papers and reports for local, state and federal government clients. She has also produced podcasts for various organisations and participated in media interviews. She has received state, national and international funding worth over USD $25 million. Usha has been awarded the Quarterly Franklin Membership by London Journals Press (UK). Her biography has been included in the Marquis Who's Who in the World® 2018, 2016 (33rd Edition), along with approximately 55,000 of the most accomplished men and women from around the world, including luminaries as U.N. Secretary-General Ban Ki-moon. In 2017, Usha was awarded the Marquis Who's Who Lifetime Achiever Award.

Meet the Volume Editor

Dr. Orhan Özçatalbaş graduated with a degree in agricultural economics from Çukurova University, Türkiye. He became an assistant professor at Akdeniz University, Türkiye, in 1998, and a professor in 2011. He is the director of the Graduate School of Natural and Applied Sciences at Akdeniz University. His research is in agricultural economics, rural development and extension, energy policy, and ICT in agriculture. In 1999–2000, he was a visiting scientist at the Institute of Horticultural Economics, Leibniz University, Hanover, Germany, as well as for courses in Italy and the Erasmus program in Poland. He has participated in many congresses in other countries. Dr. Özçatalbaş has professional experience in rural development, policy, and extension as an expert and coordinator in national and international projects. Dr. Özçatalbaş is the recipient of the 2021 Scientist of the Year Award from the Turkish Nobel Science and Research Center Association in the field of agricultural economics, especially in the field of rural tourism and development.

Contents

Preface

In the last two centuries, there has been rapid industrialization with the use of electrical energy in all fields, including agriculture, following the discovery of new inventions like steam-powered machines that convert potential energy into kinetic energy. This process has led to great changes in the residential areas of the world's population, especially in developed industrial societies, reflected by a change in the distribution of the population from rural to urban areas.

The rapid increase in the world's population, estimated to reach 10 billion in 2050, necessitates increasing food production on a global scale. According to the United Nations Food and Agriculture Organization (FAO), world food demand will increase by 70% by 2050. In addition to food insecurity, the world is experiencing climate change and global warming. The predicted effects of global warming will affect settlements, lifestyles, and production systems. As such, new production systems that are compatible with increasing temperatures brought about by global climate change should be developed.

As has been widely stated by international organizations, especially in the last few decades, "agriculture and food production are of vital importance for humanity." Climate change, environmental pollution, global warming, conflicts between nations, and the COVID-19 pandemic have once again highlighted the importance of food safety and security. Although awareness of these challenges is greater today than ever before, there is still much work to be done to increase sustainable food production. Undoubtedly, the most important work needs to be done in agricultural economics and agri-food business. Naturally, it is necessary to increase production, productivity, and resource use efficiency, ensure the minimization of inputs, ensure the optimization of agricultural-food businesses, and position the farmer and the business correctly within the sustainable life cycle.

Again, in today's current production systems, the negative effects of food safety and supply chain problems continue. In addition, mechanisms to prevent global warming are on the agenda, especially in terms of processes related to production systems and of course products subject to foreign trade, and new emission reduction rules impose additional burdens on countries. The climate change policies of EU production provide important information. For example, the regulation published in May 2023, "Carbon Border Adjustment Mechanism (CBAM)," which constitutes an important part of the European Green Deal, will also lead to a change in international trade.

It should be noted from now on that in trade and relations between countries, decisions taken against climate change, such as carbon price, carbon tax, carbon leakage, and embodied emissions, will be discussed a lot. Since the last quarter of 1990, the issue of GLOBALGAP (EUREPGAP), which is very important for food safety, has been widely discussed. This initiative is a joint quality certification program and was launched by major European retailers in 1997. Currently, with this initiative and other related initiatives, standards continue to be raised in the management of sustainable agricultural food production and marketing processes. However, as there are very impressive examples in the historical process, the agriculture and food sector is such a vital field for human life that "sometimes it is necessary to stay on track, even when the track changes."

Essentially, agricultural sciences include plant, animal, and food sciences. It encompasses production techniques, soil cultivation, soil science and plant nutrition, animal husbandry, agricultural engineering, irrigation and mechanization, plant protection, rural sociology and sustainable development, extension, forestry, natural sources, international trade, logistics, fisheries, and home economics, and of course related fields such as agricultural economics. The majority of individuals working in these scientific fields are directly related to agriculture. In addition, historians, educators, communicators, sociologists, philosophers, and pure economists have also worked and are working on agricultural sciences and issues related to rural areas.

Nowadays, concepts have diversified, agricultural sciences have developed, and multidisciplinary and interdisciplinary sciences have been formed. Important issues regarding biotechnology, bioengineering, informatics, nanotechnology, gene transfer, genetic science, sustainability, circularity, zero waste, smart and digital agriculture, precision agriculture, robots, drones, mechatronics, artificial intelligence, augmented reality, and more have been included in the process.

Agricultural economics has the role of developing practical tools to measure benefits and losses and to solve input-output optimization problems, and much emphasis has been placed on the positive benefits and costs of innovations introduced to rural areas in the agricultural economics literature. However, some economists have argued that agricultural innovation and technological change in agriculture worsen the situation of farmers. Uncontrollable threats to agriculture, such as climate change, have increased and therefore the roles of scientists and agricultural economists have become much more valuable due to the necessity of multilateral and multidisciplinary work brought about by complex structures. For this reason, there is a need to develop new methods and approaches for economic studies related to agriculture. Perhaps, in the new normal period, there is also a need to redefine the roles of the agricultural economy and agri-food business, improve their functions, and name new professions.

Changes and developments in every field and every sector make it necessary to develop new perspectives and approaches in agriculture and food science. In this context, many concepts or approaches are being derived today, along with their unique technology. New scientific findings are revealed all the time, and these findings turn into technology and provide new advantages and benefits in the resource use process. They are experiencing a period when all efforts must be met based on sustainability. A wide area is being created where new concepts emerge through R&D studies in almost every field and are transferred to sectors, and technologies are becoming widespread with participatory and inclusive models in which research and extension go together. As a result, a process in which clean or renewable energy, green and blue economy, sustainability, and circularity are harmonized continues to be constantly updated, and it seems that this will continue.

Orhan Özçatalbaş
Faculty of Agriculture,
Department of Agricultural Economics,
Institute of Natural and Applied Sciences,
Akdeniz University,
Antalya, Türkiye

Section 1

Perspectives

Chapter 1

Perspective Chapter: Exploring the Possibilities and Technologies of the Digital Agricultural Platform

Viktor Zamlynskyi, Tetyana Shabatura, Olga Zamlynska and Evgeniya Borysevych

Abstract

In connection with the significant growth of the world's population, global socioeconomic trends in the sufficiency of natural resources have become relevant. Agriculture as an industry produces food that every inhabitant of the planet consumes daily. The introduction of new technologies, while increasing efficiency, has not eliminated food shortages throughout human history. Modern digital solutions and technologies have a positive impact on productivity. Our study presents the results of a study of the big data platform and artificial intelligence for the agricultural sector, their capabilities and optimization technologies. This chapter analyzed and proposed recommendations on the quality of data analysis of agricultural processes and business administration in real time. The active introduction of digital platforms will have a positive effect on optimizing the use of resources, reducing waste and improving the efficiency of risk management and attracting investments under the conditions of transparent management of the agricultural enterprise.

Keywords: information society, smart farming, sensors, artificial intelligence, digital agricultural platform, digital agricultural technologies, sustainable agriculture management, digital farming, productivity control, precision farming, smart farming, risks, modern food production systems

1. Introduction

The digital transformation of agriculture is largely based on the integrated implementation of digital technologies within the interrelated concepts of precision farming and smart agriculture. Managing the life cycle of living beings is much more complicated than such tasks as driving a car without a driver, a voice assistant, that is, managing the "life cycle" of any inanimate object. For example, the algorithm for growing wheat is based on the interaction of natural and climatic conditions, soil fertility, seed, fertilizers, anthropogenic factor and compliance with the technological map of the growing season. Excess or lack of water and sun, the impact of pests and diseases, and cataclysms (fire, flood, drought, war, earthquake and epidemics) are difficult to predict and cannot be artificially compensated, only reduced, and the growing season cannot be suspended or moved to another place. However, the positive moment in the interaction with man and nature is that the lack of electricity and the Internet does not affect the growing season in open systems. If favorable conditions are not met during the growing season, if unsustainable agricultural methods are used, and this is a period of 3–9 months, there may be no harvest. Crop rotation, soil analysis and maintaining its fertility, temperature and precipitation dynamics over the past 100 years, analysis of global food markets and supply chains will make it possible to predict the most appropriate development strategy at different levels in modern information and communication parameters.

Despite the fact that individual elements of precision farming have been used for more than 20 years, only now integrated solutions in the fields, sustainable resource-saving crop production that combines various types of sensors, Internet of Things (IoT) technologies, automated and unmanned vehicles, robotic production systems, platform technologies for processing large data and machine learning are largely taking place.

The main task of the digital transformation of agriculture is to extract value from the collected big data about the internal and external environment. This is based on cloud platforms and big data solutions, as well as predictive analytics technologies and decision support systems. It is predicted that by 2050, the average farm will generate 4.1 million units of data (data point) per day [1].

Reducing the cost and increasing the accuracy of sensor equipment (field sensors, sensors for monitoring the condition of industrial premises, agricultural equipment and machinery, livestock health monitoring sensors, etc.) will allow a large number of agricultural enterprises to migrate to continuous collection and analysis of information and integrate three levels of monitoring of agricultural systems (ground, air, and space) at the level of individual farms, regions, and whole countries.

The digital transformation of agriculture is aimed at overcoming a number of global challenges, such as:

- increasing food demand (up to 60% by 2050) as a result of population growth and improved quality of life [2];

- depleting productive agricultural land, increasing environmental pressure (70% of water consumption and 30% of carbon dioxide emissions are currently accounted for world agriculture) and the reduction of areas suitable for agriculture;

- changes in agroclimatic conditions and an increase in the frequency of natural disasters that increase volatility in agricultural markets;

- transformation of consumer preferences and development of a sustainable and environmentally friendly consumption model.

Integrated application of precision farming technologies can provide a yield increase to 70% [3].

A prompt response to changes in external conditions and adjustment of equipment operation parameters based on incoming digital information can reduce the cost of seeds, fertilizer and fuel, and reduce time spent on field work.

Big data analytics and artificial intelligence technologies can improve the efficiency of selection processes and the development of new effective feeds and fertilizers, provide yield forecasting and select the optimal strategy for growing crops [4].

The usage of unmanned vehicles significantly reduces the cost of certain types of work. For instance, the usage of UAVs (unmanned aerial vehicles) for planting seeds can reduce the cost of this operation by 85% [1]. According to the American Farmers Association, cost reduction due to robotization of agricultural operations can reach 40% [5]. At the same time, labor productivity is also growing—for example, one robotic harvesting system can replace 30 farmworkers [5].

As a result of digitalization, consumers and regulatory authorities will have the opportunity to fully trace the origin of products [6], which will increase their safety, and will also become an additional factor in the development of consumer culture. Digital technologies will help to reduce the environmental pressure on agriculture, improve the efficiency of natural resources usage, and increase the resistance to adverse agroclimatic phenomena [7].

Digitization in agricultural sector makes it possible to achieve a number of indirect and social effects, including reducing disparities in the quality of life between urban and rural areas, ensuring the economic and social integration of smallholder farmers into food systems and supply chains (including through various marketplaces), providing rural residents with tools to increase digital literacy and expanding the set of competencies.

2. Facilities of modern technologies for digital agriculture

It is advisable to group modern technologies for digital agriculture, which are used by agro-industrial enterprises and enhance the digital transformation of agrarian production. Among these technologies, four main blocks can be distinguished:

- aerospace technologies;
- sensors and transducers;
- artificial intelligence;
- information and communication technologies.

It is necessary to analyze each block of individual digital technologies in terms of the facilities and benefits of practical use (**Table 1**).

Space technologies, including new possibilities of satellite images like space sensing and multispectral imaging, are designed to help solve the problem of precision farming. This approach involves caring for each individual square of the field through three key areas: surveillance systems, variable rate fertilization, and navigation. Namely in areas all these innovative changes that solve the main problems of agricultural enterprises in the fields and gradually draw the agro-industrial sector into the Information Technology (IT) industry are taking place.

Technology and its importance for the agricultural sector	Technology components	Possibilities
Aerospace. The basis of precision farming	Unmanned aerial vehicles, drones	• measurement of land plots; • visual control and monitoring; • liquid fertilizer application and plant protection products;
	Satellite images	• surface scanning, • multispectral shooting of agricultural lands; • guaranteed daily field monitoring;
	Geographic Information Systems (GIS)	• centralized storage and management of the cartographic database; • land management, • audit implementation of agricultural land; • control of work execution in the fields and tracking of crops in the crop's context; • evaluate the quality of soils and their potential yield;
Internet of Things (IoT). The basis for automation of production processes in the agricultural sector	Sensors and transducers	For crop production: • tracking soil parameters; • tracking plant growth parameters; • finding pests and diseases of plants; • monitoring of weather conditions; • tracking machineries in the fields. For animal husbandry: • biometrics of animals, automatic systems of feeding and maintenance of animals.
Artificial intelligence. The basis of SMART farms in the agricultural sector	Machine learning	Identification of relationships to minimize losses and increase the efficiency of production resources.
	Robotics	Automatization of repetitive operations: harvesting, weed control, pruning, sowing, sorting and packing, milking, etc.
	Big Data	• in-depth analysis of business processes in the farms of the agricultural sector to make informed management decisions; • creating a profile of a successful producer to develop an algorithm for the sustainable production of agricultural products;
Information and communication technologies. The basis of effective management and decision-making in the agricultural sector	Digital platforms, mobile applications	• remote control of agricultural land; • management of field works that need constant updating of information; • planning and forecasting of agricultural operations; • tracking the operation of equipment in the field in real time; • automation of the workflow process; • organization of a system of general access to files of an agricultural enterprise;
	Messengers, social networks	• internal communication at agricultural enterprises and farms; • exchange of experience between participants in the production process

Source: *Compiled by the authors.*

Table 1.
Modern technologies for digital agriculture.

The integrated use of space technologies in the practice of agricultural enterprises makes it possible to realize the benefits of precision farming using satellite navigation devices, space images, special software and satellite monitoring of agricultural land. The practical implementation of precision farming concept by agricultural enterprises requires the development of a decision support system, adapted to technological map of cultivation, based on the use of satellite navigation, Geographic Information Systems (GIS) technologies, remote sensing data, agricultural robotic devices and software.

The use of space technologies by agricultural enterprises makes it possible to control the development of plants. With the help of satellite images, it is possible to build maps of plant development (Normalized Difference Vegetation Index (NDVI) maps), determine relief features of the enterprise land bank and the agrochemical composition of the soil cover, which makes it possible to apply different agricultural technologies to each section of the field.

The next block of digital agriculture technologies consists of various sensors and transducers that are used to automate production processes in the agricultural sector.

The employment of intelligent sensors and transducers, whose job it is to gather data about the environment and agriculture in real time, is directly tied to the majority of the production activities that comprise modern precision farming.

In precision farming, sensors and transducers are categorized into five classes.

The first group of sensors and transducers provides the maximum accuracy of crop yield monitoring based on the measurement of the following parameters:

- weather conditions (measurement of wind speed and direction, amount of precipitation);
- soil morphology (water potential, temperature and oxygen level in the soil);
- the need for fertilizers (determining the required amount of fertilizers by measuring electrical resistance);
- solar radiation (measurement of ultraviolet and short-wave radiation, radiation for photosynthesis);
- plant growth (dendrometers to control the growth of the root, stem and fruit).

The second group consists of agricultural sensors for determining the vegetation of plants with high accuracy. Usually, a video camera with such sensors is installed on a drone or an unmanned aerial vehicle. It can collect real-time visual data of the condition of crops in the fields, and it helps agronomists to identify problems with crops at an early stage and with great accuracy.

The third group consists of sensors for determining the soil, which analyze its condition and the required amount of water in it. The feature of the soil sensors is the ability to determine the necessity for watering in different parts of the field. This prevents waterlogging and washing out of useful microelements during artificial irrigation.

The fourth group consists of sensors that allow you to monitor the presence of pests in a certain part of the field. If the identified indicators exceed the critical number of the pest population, then the information is transmitted to the agronomist to make a decision on the localization or elimination of this problem.

The fifth group of sensors are digital IoT tools that allow you to accumulate all the information from the first four groups. They process incoming information and ensure the timeliness of its processing for management response and troubleshooting.

All of these digital technological solutions are sources of information, so there is a need to process and analyze a large amount of information in order to make effective decisions and develop forecasts. For such information processing, Big Data technologies are used, which are the main elements of modern SMART farms in the agricultural sector. In the making of data processing, machine learning (ML) technologies are used, which, based on the analysis of large information amounts, reveal new relationships in the activities of agricultural enterprises, which allow us to make informed management decisions.

Artificial intelligence (AI) technologies that are used in agriculture have a number of significant features:

- these are technical solutions, primarily software and hardware tools for performing certain agricultural work or forecasting the development of the agricultural sector, depending on various factors (climate, soil conditions, rainfall and market prices). Often AI technologies are used in conjunction with robotics, here we can talk about their interaction. So, the robot provides movement, manipulation of objects and tools, and AI technologies, in turn, carry out orientation in space, choose the optimal tools for the robot when performing a certain task and also help to recognize obstacles and objects;

- these technologies are used for agriculture, i.e., directly in the production of food or the development of an optimal agricultural management strategy. This means the need to take into account the functioning in changing natural and climatic conditions; working with living organisms—plants, animals; and functioning in livestock buildings or open areas, which makes it necessary to navigate in space, often with pattern recognition (various unsorted objects);

- these technologies perform intellectual functions in the implementation of work in agriculture, which consist in the ability to carry out abstract conclusions, act in conditions of incomplete information and show the ability to self-learn.

Information and communication technologies are actively used in agriculture nowadays and include the use of digital platforms, mobile applications, instant messengers and social networks.

3. Cloud technologies as the foundation for building digital platforms

Nowadays, technologies for providing information and communication services are being improved continuously, opening up new opportunities for business. The most promising and flexible are modern "cloud" and "cloud computing" technologies.

The "cloud" technology model is a complex infrastructure that is created on the basis of building a data center (a building that houses server and network equipment with Internet access channels) [8].

The National Institute of Standards and Technology (NIST) defined in the document "NIST Definition of Cloud Computing v15" [9] the cloud computing technology model as follows: the cloud computing model enables convenient network access on demand to cloud functions using communication channels.

The cloud model is characterized by five main features:

- service on demand;
- wide network access;
- pooled resource;
- independent location;
- fast flexibility, changeable services.

Today, there is a choice of four cloud hosting models Functions as a Service (FaaS), Platform-as-a-Service (PaaS), Software as a Service (SaaS) or Infrastructure as a Service (IaaS), which is based on traditional data centers [10]. It should be noted that in fact, this is mostly a choice of three options, since the FaaS model is still experimental both for online trading and for other business areas. In general, choosing a FaaS, PaaS, SaaS or IaaS cloud model to build, for example, a digital business platform is a decision with many criteria, and each model has its pros and cons depending on business practices and the properties of the software itself (**Figure 1**) [11].

As part of the IaaS model (Infrastructure as a Service), the data center provides dedicated servers or virtual machines, as well as data storage and network connectivity to backbone Internet links. The client (customer of the service model), for instance, a large agricultural company pays for the services of the provider according to the operating expenses model (OpEx) [12] depending on the current consumption of Pay-As-You-Go, or, in other words, as a subscription. This payment method frees

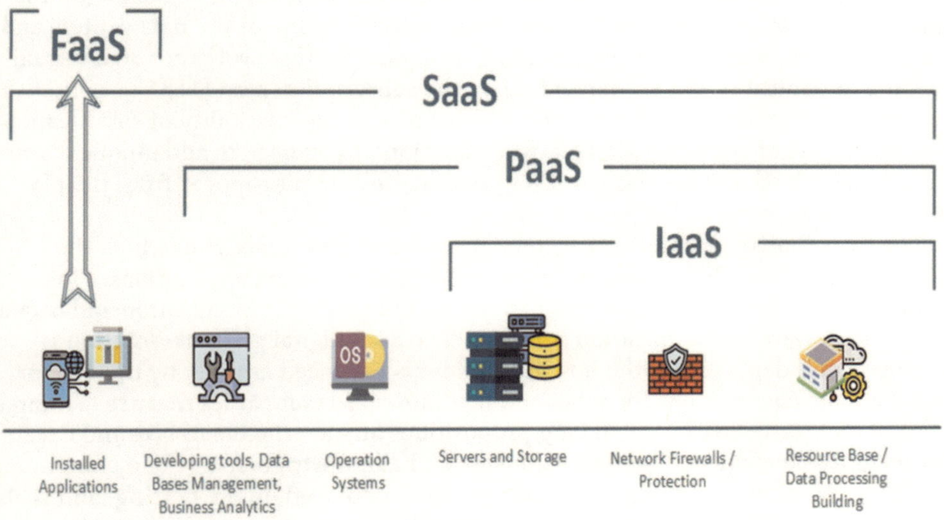

Figure 1.
Cloud hosting models for organizing digital platforms. Image source: *Modified by the authors based on [11].*

the budget of the agricultural company from capital expenditures (CapEx) for the purchase of its own servers and other IT equipment. That payment method is applicable to any of the cloud models FaaS, PaaS, SaaS or IaaS [10, 13].

The advantage of the IaaS model is a fairly high level of control over equipment and applications, especially if the agricultural company has a professional IT team. However, on the other hand, this is also a disadvantage, since the company bears the costs of paying programmers, network engineers and network administrators. If the IT staff of the agricultural company makes mistakes while configuring the servers, storages, network stacks, installing or updating software, the agricultural company incurs losses due to denials in servicing user requests [10].

In modern data centers, the IaaS cloud model allows you to flexibly scale leased IT resources in accordance with the progress of projects, increase or decrease in load. Unlike other models of cloud services (FaaS, PaaS or SaaS), a feature of IaaS is the provision of leasing only physical devices and a network connection to the Internet. The software for the IaaS model is installed by the customer company independently, and the data center is not responsible for the operation of these applications [10, 13].

The IaaS model is used primarily in the field of e-commerce, and it is most suitable for online stores and marketplaces, where owners want to have control over their business's IT infrastructure, website and other online applications, but do not want to invest a lot of money in creating their own data center (or server room) [13].

In the PaaS (Platform-as-a-Service) model, there are changes in the composition of the leased infrastructure. It is no longer provided only as a set of servers, but also provides preinstalled operating systems for the client's choice, tools for creating, testing and running applications. The convenience of the PaaS model is that the client does not need to administer system software. There is complete freedom in which applications, software and development tools are deployed on the leased infrastructure. The client can create and upload his own code, install and administer databases.

Using the PaaS model, the vendor, in addition to the actual sale of services and platform applications, also provides services for its installation on its hosting in the data center. In other words, the vendor rents capacity in one of the data centers and creates a script for automatically installing its digital platform software on a virtual machine or dedicated server, depending on the subscription plan [11].

In the PaaS model, the client of this service retains the possibility of significant customization of the basic digital platform solution. If you need to add unique features to implement business processes without waiting for them to appear from the platform provider, then PaaS is the best choice [10, 13].

The SaaS (Software as a Service) model is a cloud-based model in which the provider takes over all the tasks of deploying and maintaining applications. This includes cloud server hosting, operating system installation, virtualization and backup tools, middleware and application software. The SaaS digital platform solution is developed and deployed on the hosting, and is also serviced entirely by the vendor. This is a huge convenience for small and medium-sized companies that are looking to get to market faster with their selling propositions and are unable to hire an IT team that includes developers, network engineers and administrators.

The application according to the SaaS model is deployed on the hosting, and is also serviced entirely by the vendor. This is a great convenience for small to medium businesses. Business users can buy access to SaaS digital platform services (applications) directly from a web browser (or mobile device) [10, 13].

Functions as a Service (FaaS) represents a new level of abstraction, in which the physical and software architecture completely disappears, except for individual "functions" that are called when there is a need for their execution. A function in FaaS has the highest level of abstraction as the smallest component (brick) of a large application. Although FaaS is often fully associated with serverless computing, it is correct to speak about FaaS as a software part or software component of serverless computing, as viewed from the user's point of view [14].

With FaaS, a development team can break down their application into separate functions and upload them to the FaaS platform. Such platforms are offered by global cloud service providers—Microsoft Azure, AWS Lambda, IBM Cloud Functions and Google Cloud Functions.

The FaaS model is very economical, since the customer of the service pays only for the server time required to call and execute functions, but in reality, this is true only for purely computational tasks. Today, this model is still not widespread enough [14].

In cases where the basic functionality of a SaaS solution does not satisfy the customer of the service, and even applications that extend the functionality (add-ons) cannot help, a digital platform offered under the PaaS cloud model should be preferred. This is especially true for the B2B (business-to-business) market, where there may be special conditions in the selling of goods that require unique platform customization using the PaaS or even the IaaS model [10, 13].

The boundaries between available resources in each model (PaaS, SaaS and IaaS) may vary slightly across cloud providers. In an effort to provide maximum coverage of customer needs, providers are blurring the boundaries between cloud hosting models by adding services from adjacent models. The traditional areas of responsibility of the client and the service provider are shown in **Figure 2**.

The PaaS model is most often in demand for large and medium-sized businesses, as it achieves an excellent balance between the convenience of platform administration and access to code, virtualization, server configurations and databases.

Modern digital platforms are built on the considered models of cloud services and perform a wide variety of tasks in all sectors of the economy, including agriculture.

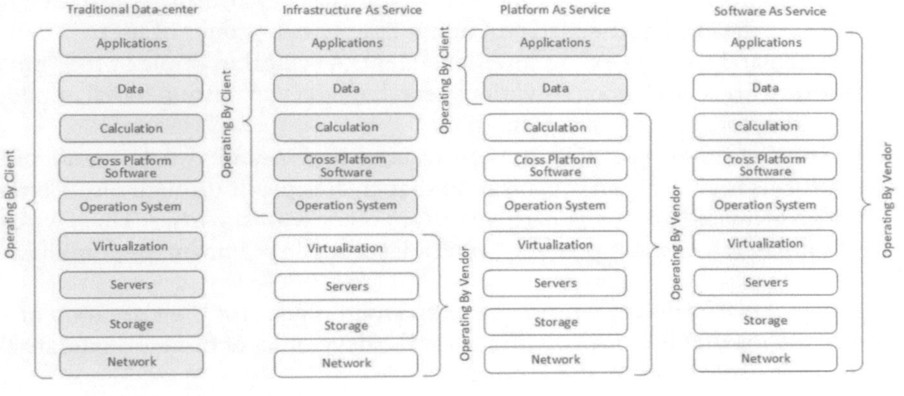

Figure 2.
Distribution of traditional areas of responsibility of the client and the service provider for different cloud service models. Image source: Modified by the authors.

4. Attribute-based structuring of digital platforms

The European Commission defines digital platforms, focusing on their functional purpose, such as: search engines, social networks, e-commerce platforms, app purchase stores, price comparison sites, etc. [15].

Of course, this definition, despite its recent origin, is now already outdated, although, as in the case of the concept of "digital services," the definition of "digital platforms" still needs to be clarified.

In the literature, there are many definitions of "digital platforms" concept which are either too complex or too simplistic, but provide an opportunity to define the key attributes of the platforms. It is indicated that a digital platform is a technology-enabled business model that facilitates the exchange of information between information users and their consumers, who do not necessarily know each other, thereby achieving a certain confidentiality (trust).

According to researchers [16], a digital platform is a complex information system that provides a specific way to perform a certain function and is open for use by customers and partners, including application developers, merchants and agents. The platform can be used directly or through applications created on its basis with the owner or third parties [16].

A digital platform, as was pointed out by P. Evans and A. Gower [17], is a technology, product or service that is both a transactional and an innovative platform. This category includes companies, such as Apple, which have an App Store trading platform and a large ecosystem of independent developers who create content on the platform.

As a rule, digital platforms consist of a stable main component and a set of several additional components—services that provide the "attractiveness" of the platform for customers. The main component is connected to additional services using an interface. On the main component, an add-on is built from additional service components. Developers of additional services also use the appropriate interfaces to communicate with the main platform. In this regard, researchers [17] define a platform as building blocks that act as a basis on which firms, sometimes called a business ecosystem, can develop additional products, technologies or services.

There is an opinion that the digital platform is a means of organizing information exchange in the digital economy by concentrating information and further distributing it on the network. In this sense, the term "multilateral platform" is also used to define it, i.e., it means that the platform unites at least two groups of users, interconnected and to some extent interdependent. A typical example of the "multilateral platform" business model is various search engines that bring together people who are looking for this or that information.

In the work of the authors [18], a more accurate and meaningful definition of digital platforms is given as an organization that creates profit through direct interaction between affiliated groups of participants, in other words, parties. Thus, we can say that multilateral, or more precisely, multiplayer mode is a hallmark of multilateral platforms.

Also, digital platforms are considered as an environment for the formation of digital ecosystems that provide conditions for the development of new digital markets and demand for new services and services.

The above definitions make it possible to single out the main attributes inherent in digital platforms, on the basis of which it is possible to give a generalized definition of this concept (**Table 2**).

Attribute	Attribute content
Purpose	Information concentration and its distribution
Object	Set of digital data, digital services
Actors (Subjects)	Set of interested users
Location	Information network space
Ownership	Platform creator
Access method	Remote
Economic sense for the user	Reducing transaction costs due to the availability of information, the use of digital technologies and services
Economic sense for the owner	Income from rent for the usage of a digital platform and fees for access to resources

Source: *Compiled by the authors.*

Table 2.
Attribute-based structuring of digital platforms.

5. Types of digital platforms and examples of typology for agriculture

In the research of P. Evans and A. Gaver [17], it has been attempted to create a typology of currently existing platforms. The authors distinguish three types of platforms.

1. Transaction platforms are a technology, product or service that acts as an information channel that facilitates transactions, as well as information exchange between market participants.

2. An innovation platform is a technology, product or service that is the technological basis for providing services to other companies that develop their own technologies, products and services.

3. An integrated platform is a technology, product or service that can be considered both as a transactional and as an innovative platform, i.e., providing transactional opportunities and facilitating the work of other innovative firms.

It is advisable to give examples of the types of platforms that are created for the agricultural sector.

Recently, the PaaS model has been actively entering into the practice of agricultural enterprises. In this model, the customer is given the opportunity to use the cloud infrastructure to host the basic software, as well as new or existing user services (his own, custom-made or purchased). These user services are readymade procedures and solutions for various practical tasks.

For instance, the services of the largest digital platform for agricultural sector Cropwise (Syngenta Group) are providing such software modules [19]:

1. *Cropwise Protector* is a digital tool that makes agronomy decisions easier and faster by turning data into meaningful insights.

2. *Cropwise Sustainability* – ensuring sustainable agriculture for the large-scale production, certification, and sale of food grown in compliance with the principles of sustainable development.

3. *Cropwise Operation* is a comprehensive solution for monitoring the condition of fields and crops in one place in real time.

4. *Cropwise Commodity Pro* – protecting future premium crop volume from falling commodity prices during the growing season.

5. *Cropwise Seed Selector* – recommendations for choosing seeds to help consultant agronomists and agricultural producers.

6. *Cropwise Planting* – accounting for intrafield variability, optimizing the use of resources for each field, getting the most out of hybrids and increasing profitability.

7. *Cropwise Imagery* – images to monitor the status of crops anytime, anywhere.

8. *Cropwise Spray Assist* – helps specialists choose the best methods on the job.

Thus, the usage of the services of such a digital platform allows the user (farmer, farm or agricultural enterprise) to effectively solve their production problems. The user can choose a set of services to support a specific production situation. It is advisable to classify such a platform as a transactional one.

The development and improvement of digital platforms for the agricultural sector is an ongoing process.

Food and Agriculture Organization (FAO) has developed applications, databases and platforms to support the work being carried out in countries around the world [20]. These digital services increase access to useful data, information, digital maps and statistics.

One of the most significant geospatial platforms for accelerating agricultural transformation and sustainable rural development to eradicate poverty (Sustainable Development Goal 1 (SDG1)) and eliminate hunger and all forms of malnutrition (Sustainable Development Goal 2 (SDG2)) is the Hand-in-Hand (HiH) geospatial platform. This platform contributes to the achievement of all sustainable development goals.

Hand-in-Hand has brought together over 20 FAO units across multiple domains, from Animal Health to Trade and Markets, integrating data from across FAO on Soil, Land, Water, Climate, Fisheries, Livestock, Crops, Forestry, Trade, Social and Economics. At the moment, a million geospatial layers have been collected, thousands of statistics series with 4000 metadata records.

In addition, popular digital tools offered by FAO are [20]:

1. WAPOR, a portal to monitor Water Productivity through open access of remotely sensed derived data;

2. Crop Calendar, a tool that provides timely information about seeds to promote local crop production. It contains information on planting, sowing and harvesting periods of locally adapted crops in specific agroecological zones. It

also provides information on the sowing rates of seed and planting material and the main agricultural practices.

3. Food Price Monitoring and Analysis (FPMA), this web portal contains the latest information and analysis on domestic prices of basic foods mainly in developing countries. It provides early warning on high food prices at country level that may negatively affect food security.

4. Agricultural Stress Index System (ASIS), it monitors agricultural areas with a high likelihood of water stress/drought at global, regional and country levels, using satellite-based remote sensing data at 1 km resolution. It simulates the analysis that remote sensing experts and agronomists would undertake and simplifies the usage and interpretation of the data for a broader audience.

5. FAMEWS, through the FAMEWS app and its platform, data on Fall Armyworm can be collected at the farm level and collated for sharing at local, national and global levels to manage the pest, identify priority areas and foster early warning mechanisms for all stakeholders.

Given the nature of the digital services developed by FAO, such a digital platform can be classified as innovative.

An example of an integrated platform can be the platform Datahub created under the leadership of the Data Center of the Kenya Agricultural and Livestock Research Organization (KALRO), which integrated [21]:

- the platform of The National Potato Council of Kenya (NPCK) Viazi Soko, provides seeds, market links and information exchange for participants in the potato value chain with plans to expand through the aggregation of multiple digital services and logistics.

- The Agricultural Transformation Agency (ATA) is a government agency pioneering multiple digital agriculture projects in Ethiopia with outreach to more than 5 million farmers.

The Datahub offers a suite of eight open-source digital services that cater to ecosystem actors, field organizations and farmers, and financial service providers by packaging data insights into ways that easily translate to their needs.

Digital platform actors (e.g., donors and governments) receive verified field data to inform planning and improve insights from existing models. Field organizations (e.g., tech innovators and research organizations) and farmers get agronomic information to increase farmer productivity and improve their income. Financial service providers (e.g., banks and insurance companies) receive aggregated farmer data to inform loan decisions and insurance payouts.

Services of the integrated platform KALRO-NPCK-ATA [21] are as given follows:

1. Food balance sheet (FBS) tracks Kenya's food supply and demand, incorporating yield estimates for planning.

2. Livestock/crop suitability mapping, maps areas that are suited to specific crops and livestock.

3. 3) Modeling environmental changes, models climate change effects on agriculture ecosystems.

4. Early warning alert, signals impending disasters, food market, interruptions and their expected scale.

5. Weather/crop monitoring, provides weather forecasts and agronomic advice to farmers based on a crop location.

6. Livestock/crop selector, advises farmers on crop and livestock breeds based on map suitability

7. Agri-coach, advises farmers on the whole value chain building on inputs from other digital projects.

8. Credit scoring, assigns credit scores to farmers to access credit, leveraging agri-coach metrics.

The value proposition of the services 1–3 consists of using accurate field data to inform national planning, program development and help improve the analysis of existing models. The stakeholders in these products are politicians, donors and satellite companies.

The value propositions of the services 4–8 of the digital platform Datahub consist of providing actionable agronomic information to farmers and agronomic organizations so as to increase productivity and profitability, as well as to provide data on the activities of farmers for informing their decision to issue bank loans. The stakeholders in these products are technological innovators, research organizations, farmers, financial service providers, banks and insurance.

6. Digital platform: The decision support system tool for smart farming

A fairly large number of tools for decision support systems (DSS) for smart agriculture (Smart Farming) are currently used in agriculture. Digital platforms are one of the most effective tools for DSS, as they are data aggregators, perform the function of systematization and analysis of these data. Based on this analysis and using modern technologies, services are created that allow both small farms and large agro-industrial complexes to make informed management decisions.

Digital technologies, such as the Internet of Things (IoT) and machine learning (ML) methods, are opening up new opportunities for agriculture. These technologies include data sharing, homogenization, the ability to edit, reprogram and distribute data, meaning that no single participant has complete ownership of the data. A key element in creating value using these technologies is data, namely Big Data [22].

Data can come from different sources, for example:

- farmers and small farms;
- large agro-industrial complexes;
- satellite images;

- national agricultural statistics services; and
- thematic groups in social networks.

Such data, processed on a digital platform and presented in a user-friendly format, can greatly enhance the ability of agricultural producers to interact with suppliers and buyers.

However, producers will only be willing to share such data as long as their personal benefit outweighs the cost of such sharing. Here, an important role is played by such factors as the safety of using information for its source, the intentions of the interested party regarding the information received and the rules that exist in the issue of limiting the value that is created from the received data.

Data are the main assets of a digital platform, a fungible commodity that a farmer offers in exchange for more valuable information. The platform must collect and store data to support value creation, where the total value created will be the product of the benefit generated by the data, the benefit created by the system itself and the benefit generated by the user community [23].

All data from different sources can be combined into a single space and available in a certain form for information processing. There are features that a big data aggregator service must comply with:

- updating information should be accurate and as automatic as possible, which is necessary for building predictive models;
- the amount of incoming data should be large and always up to date;
- the cloud service must ensure the safety and reliability of saving Big Data.

Such requirements are met with, for example, by the cloud service Amazon Web Services (AWS), which is the most widespread among users of digital platforms [24].

The following model of a digital agricultural data platform can be proposed, as shown in **Figure 3**.

This model has three layers:

1. The layer of objects, in which the data come from different sources and then structures.
2. The management layer, in which the data are unified and standardized, then processed and formed DSS (decision support system).
3. The layer of value creation, which presents the services of the digital platform available to its users.

It should be noted that the construction of DSS is based on ML (Machine Learning) algorithms, which are processed in the operational core, based on cloud computing and the results can be, for example, forecasting, warning and anomaly detection.

Thus, it is obvious that digital agricultural platforms while operating add value to data and allow creating an effective DSS, which is presented to users in the form of various digital services: WWW (World Wide Web), applications and digital maps. Such a DSS can help, for example, farmers to make smart decisions, such as organizing

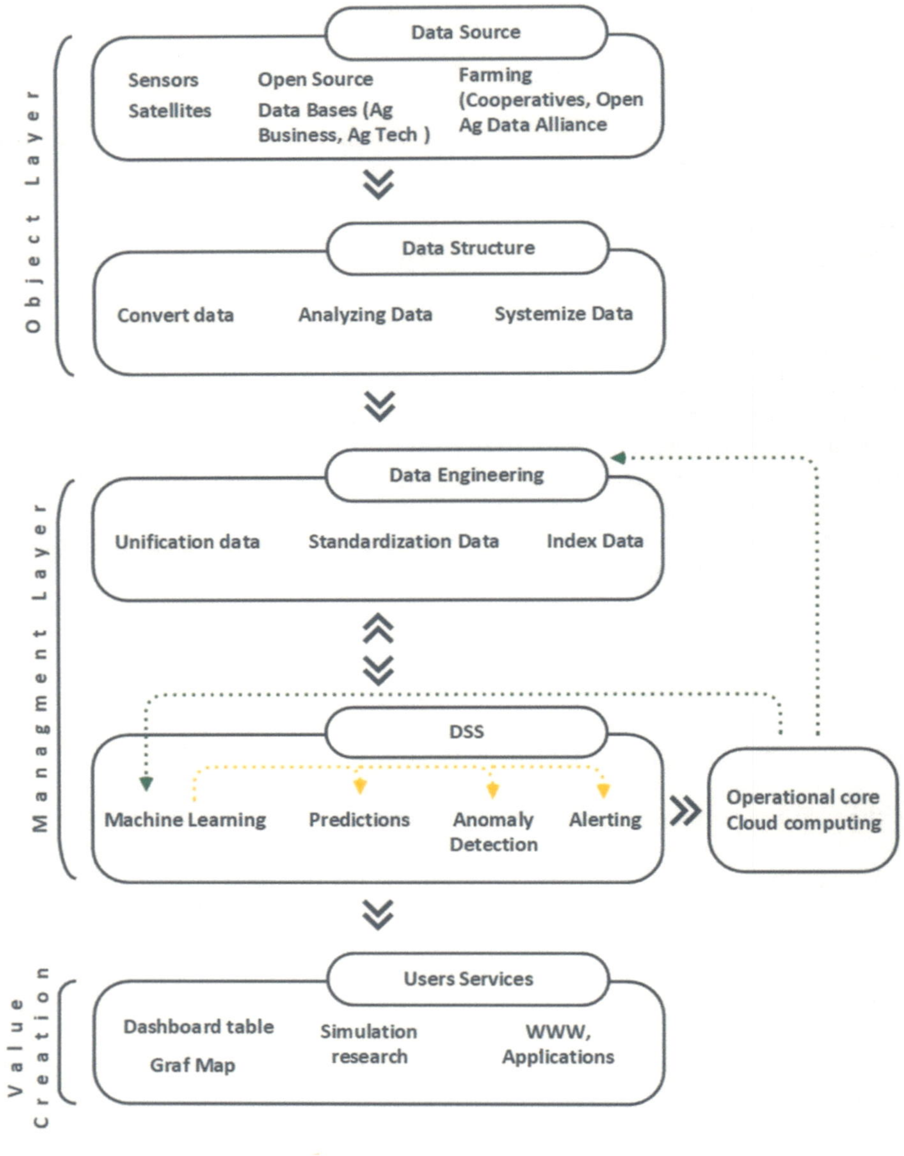

Figure 3.
Model of the digital agricultural data platform. Image source: *Developed by the authors.*

the optimal irrigation process, managing the process of feeding crops with nutrients and making decisions about the rational feeding of animals [25].

However, in the process of practical use of such a digital agricultural data platform model, the following problems inevitably arise:

- ensuring trust and security in the process of data exchange;
- integration of a sufficiently large number of manufacturers that provide information;

- obtaining decisions and recommendations that are of significant importance in the process of agricultural activity.

The practical functioning of such a model requires the willingness of all participants to exchange data. In practice, however, this willingness is not always present. For example, farmers, farmer organizations that provide raw data do not have the right to analyze it, and also do not have the right to control the distribution of income that is received from the created data value (value creation) [26].

The following problem arises: since there is no complete transparency in the use of the data that are provided, in certain cases a potential source of information does not want to share its data that have been developed in the course of practical activities. In this case, the problem can be solved by providing, for example, interested parties, such as farmers, some digital platform services for free to encourage them to share data.

And this practice is actively used by service developers. For example, the Farmable service [27] is designed to manage an agricultural farm. Farmable is a service designed to help solve the specific production needs of producers of fruits, berries and fruits of other tree crops. The service can work on different devices, namely mobile devices, tablets and computers, thanks to a combination of different applications and additional modules.

The developers have optimized the application to help in the production of such types of products as: fruits (apples, pears), pome and stone fruits, nuts (almonds and macadamia nuts), berries (strawberries, blueberries, blackberries), grapes and vineyards, olives and avocados. The service modules are shown in **Figure 4**.

Farmable Core modules in **Figure 4** are marked in green and they are provided to users free of charge. Additional modules, such as Safe Spraying, Reporting and Sales Management, are provided for a fee (price from 19 to 199€ per year for one farm).

It is advisable to propose the following recommendations to ensure the effectiveness of the functioning of digital agricultural platforms using Big Data:

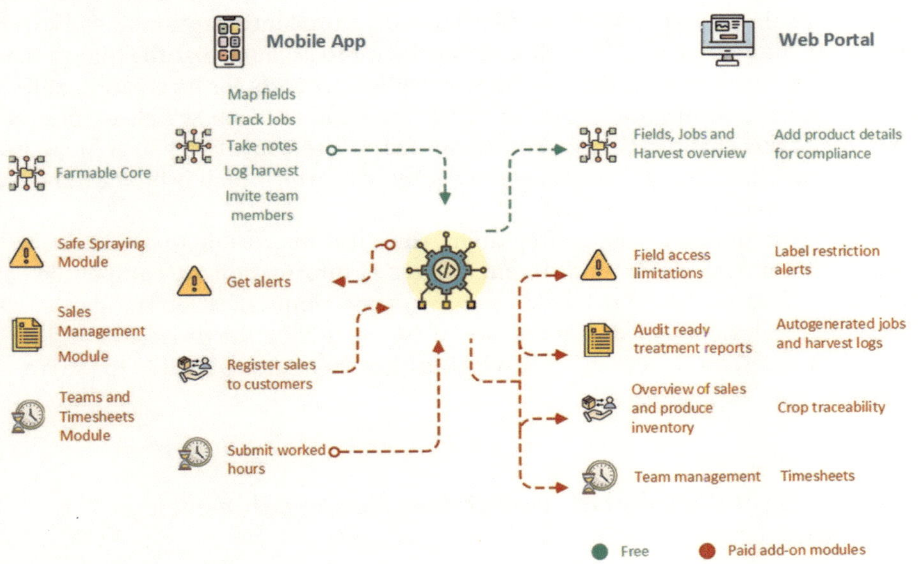

Figure 4.
Functional modules of the farmable service. Image source: *Modified by the authors based on [27].*

1. It is necessary to ensure the trust in data and the transparency of their use by interested parties. This requires clear conditions (contractual and legal) for access to the use of these data. It is also necessary to provide stakeholders with information on how these data will be used and how the value created will be distributed.

2. It is necessary to establish rules and conditions for the use of data. To do this, it is necessary to define and describe the ownership of data, the conditions for user access to specific data and the mechanism for their use.

3. It is necessary to indicate to stakeholders the types of incentives that will be offered for providing private data, so that all participants in the digital agricultural platform receive fair benefits from using the platform services.

4. It is necessary to ensure data monetization. To do this, it is necessary to develop a mechanism for determining the value of personal advice, which is obtained on the basis of DSS generation. To motivate stakeholders to use the services of the digital platform, it is recommended to provide part of the services for free.

From the point of view of the quality of data analysis, the main problems here are data preservation and standardization, data scarcity and their integration.

Some data may be stored for a long time and used for a long time. To ensure the safety of data when designing a data center (**Figure 3**), equipment developers use the appropriate standards, for example, the TIA-942 standard ("Telecommunications Infrastructure Standard for Data Center" [28], which provides a given fault tolerance.

For example, the TIA-942 standard defines four levels of data-center uptime. The first tier, Tier 1, is the lowest, at 99.67%, which corresponds to a planned downtime of 28.8 h per year. The highest level of fault tolerance is recorded in the data center of the fourth class (Tier 4), it is at 99.995%, which means a total interruption in work of no more than 15 min per year [28]. It should be taken into account that the higher the level of fault tolerance of the data center, the higher the costs for its creation and operation, and as a result, the higher the tariffs for cloud services, which are described in Section 3 of this chapter. Consequently, this factor also contributes to an increase in the costs of maintaining and operating the digital platform, which is built on the basis of these cloud services.

A rather difficult issue is data integration, since it is impossible to determine in advance whether data sets from different sources of information are compatible with each other. This issue can be resolved using two-way communication standards [29].

Thus, digital agricultural data platforms allow organizing the process of adding value to data based on the use of DSS, which makes them indispensable for smart agriculture (Smart Farming).

7. Possibilities of digital platform services for the value cycle in agriculture

Digital agricultural data platforms improve the speed of data processing and efficiency of formation of initial indicators, control and provide environmental sustainability of the entire global agro-industrial system, as they reduce transaction costs and prevent disruptions in the sale of products, improving the quality of analysis in proportion to the amount of information aggregated.

The efficiency of the agro-industrial system is increased by reducing the cost of copying, transporting and searching for data, strengthening the integration and interconnection between all participants in the production process. As the marginal cost of delivering digital information approaches zero, it reduces the digital asymmetry, thus shortening the agricultural value chain. Digital platforms facilitate market alignment between producers and consumers, borrowers and lenders, resource providers and product manufacturers, thanks to data analysis information systems, software products, computer technology and related data processing techniques.

The use of digital platforms reduces disparities in access to agricultural information, expands the scope of financial services and provides access to global markets. With low search, transaction and verification costs, digital agricultural data platforms improve access to credit, finance and insurance.

Currently, one of the key tasks of world agriculture is to ensure its sustainable development [30]. Improving the sustainable use of water, land and biodiversity resources while improving food security and productivity growth is critical to ensuring enough food for a growing world population. Digital agricultural data platforms help producers (farmers and agricultural holdings) optimize the use of land and water. Built on a digital platform, storage capabilities enable producers to reduce wastage of resources and minimize negative external environmental impacts, including greenhouse gas emissions, soil erosion and fertilizer runoff, while at the same time increasing crop yields.

To determine the impact of digital platform services on the value creation process in agriculture, it is logical to group all stakeholders involved in this process into four groups. These groups are formed in accordance with the value creation cycle in agriculture (**Figure 5**):

- Input hub.
- Production hub.
- Postharvest hub.
- Consumer hub.

Each hub has certain resources that help solve problems that arise during the implementation of the value cycle.

Examples of agricultural information digital platform services are shown in **Table 3**.

Input hub services help agricultural producers provide greater access to quality inputs (seeds and fertilizers). This happens due to the optimization of disparate networks of agrodealers, elimination of the negative effect of lack of information, which is relevant primarily for small farms.

An example of such a service is myAgro, a service in Senegal and Mali that helps smallholders acquire quality agricultural inputs based on milestone payments through a mobile phone platform. By topping up their myAgro accounts, farmers save money and then pay for it over time through the application.

Figure 5.
Functions of digital platform services in the context of the value cycle in agriculture. Source: *Developed by the authors.*

Direction number According to Figure 5	Service name, link	
	International	National
1.1	myAgro https://www.myagro.org/	Lima Links Zambia http://www.limalinkszambia.com/
1.2	Hello Tractor https://hellotractor.com/	Tun Yat Myanmar https://www.tunyat.com/
1.3	Agunity https://www.agunity.com/	MyCrop Indonesia https://mycrop.tech/
1.4	Syngenta https://www.syngenta.com/	M-pesa Kenya https://www.safaricom.co.ke
1.5	neoInt https://www.neoint.ai/	QualiTrace Ghana http://www.qualitrace.com/
2.1	FarmERP https://www.farmerp.com/	Poladrone Malaysia https://www.aonic.com/my/
2.2	Sailog https://agrio.app	Sipindo Indonesia https://sipindo.id/

Direction number According to Figure 5	Service name, link	
	International	National
2.3	Digital Green https://www.digitalgreen.org/	Farmerline Ghana https://farmerline.co/
2.4	N-Finds https://andfrnds.com/	AgriProFocus Netherlands https://agriprofocus.com/agriprofocus
3.1	One Acre Fund https://oneacrefund.org/	DATAGRO Brazil https://www.datagro.com/
3.2	TruTrade http://www.trutradeafrica.net/	Twiga Kenya https://twiga.com/
3.3	Logistimo https://logistimo.com/	Selina Wamucii https://www.selinawamucii.com/
3.4	Agromovil https://www.agromovil.co/	Kumwe Rwanda https://www.kumwe.com/
3.5	Farmcloud http://www.farmcloud.io/	Choupal Saagars India https://www.itcportal.com/businesses/agri-business/e-choupal.aspx
3.6	Stellapps https://www.stellapps.com/	Olam Cameroon https://www.olamgroup.com/
4.1	Evigence https://evigence.com/	BactuSense Israel https://www.f6s.com/company/bactusensetechnologies
4.2	Scantrust https://www.scantrust.com/	Shellcatch Chile https://web.shellcatch.com/
4.3	TruTrade http://www.trutradeafrica.net/	Rego Pantes Indonesia https://regopanties.id/

Source: *compiled by the authors.*

Table 3.
*Service examples (according to **Figure 5**).*

For sustainable farming, farm mechanization plays a key role, as it allows you to increase yields, optimize the workplace, increase profitability and at the same time reduce the risks associated with climatic conditions. Digital platforms can provide farm equipment rental services, allowing small farmers to reap the benefits of mechanization.

Tun Yat digital platform services (Myanmar) connects farmers who want to rent agricultural equipment with equipment suppliers (large or small). Tun Yat offers affordable and reliable tractor and harvester rental services.

With services that verify the quality and authenticity of the resources are used, agricultural producers can protect their brands and maintain the trust of their customers. Services created on the basis of using blockchain technology employ verification methods such as scan codes that allow you to detect fake resources.

For example, the neoInt service uses tracking technology to authenticate resources and fight counterfeit products. neoInt not only performs authentication, but also provides analytics tools to track products as they move from one stage to the next, until the end consumer also checks the source and quality of the product.

Production hub services help agricultural producers to carry out the production process more efficiently. Service products of digital agricultural platforms can improve the yield and quality of agricultural products in precision farming, increasing economic sustainability.

For instance, Poladrone (Malaysia) provides drones and field mapping services that allow farmers to calculate yields and detect trees or crops affected by diseases or pests. Farmers can use these field maps to improve their farming accuracy. In addition, using field coordinates obtained through the service, drones can also treat individual diseased plants with a pesticide sprayer attached to the drone.

Saillog is an international company, which offers Agrio, an AI-powered service that allows farmers to identify and treat plant diseases and pests. Agrio is a free interactive app for smart phones. Agrio users upload images of their diseased crops, which are then analyzed using an artificial intelligence algorithm to automatically identify diseases. Users can receive a response to their request within seconds, while they can also share their images with a team of experts who will provide recommendations on effective plant treatments.

Postharvest hub services facilitate the exchange of information regarding markets and prices for agricultural products, which is of great importance during the harvest season. These services make it easier and faster to establish links between product manufacturers and their potential customers, thereby reducing revenue losses due to insufficient and timely market information.

With the help of the DATAGRO (Brazil) service, agricultural producers can get an individual assessment of their market niche. This assessment includes competitors' production forecasts, customer requests, price estimates and logistics risks.

The services of the international digital platform Agromovil (Latin America and Africa) connect manufacturers and carriers of products, as well as markets, forming a single chain from "farm to market." When the harvest is ready for sale, producers contact buyers through the Agromovil application of the same name, and carriers carry out group export of the crop to increase the efficiency of each trip.

An interesting service, Choupal Saagars (India), was developed by ITC to improve the efficiency of processing and storage systems for agricultural products. Choupal Saagars are Internet kiosks that allow Indian farmers to access market information, including details about the collection and storage of agricultural products. Moreover, the service offers a unique virtual rural marketplace, providing a wide range of products beneficial to farmers. It also offers information and consultations related to the production of agricultural goods and even extends to banking.

Consumer hub services help to ensure the safety of consumption of both raw and processed agricultural products through tracking systems and the detection of spoiled products. These systems allow to solve such problems as poor access of products to the market and insufficient monitoring of product quality. These services help ensure that food products are handled and processed correctly, improving quality and reducing food waste.

BactuSense (Israel) has developed an innovative patented technology for the rapid detection and quantification of bacteria in food and water samples. Instead of the 48–72 h incubation periods required for Petri dishes, the Bac-Tracker gives the same results after 3–5 h with a 97% correlation. The service is easy to use and can be installed next to any food production line. The use of this technology makes it possible to optimize supply chains and ensure the release of products in the shortest possible time with guaranteed quality, which significantly reduces the manufacturer's storage costs.

As can be seen from the above, services can contribute to the growth of agricultural entrepreneurship, especially when the right enabling environment is in place. In addition, such services help agricultural producers make rational management decisions that can ensure sustainable agricultural production.

Nowadays, many development companies offer a variety of interesting digital services to ensure sustainable agricultural production.

For example, Source Trace (a SaaS company) has developed the DATAGREEN platform, which provides comprehensive solutions for managing all aspects of the agricultural value chain [31]. The DATAGREEN (DG) Agri Solution software consists of modules (**Figure 6**) that are designed to meet the specific requirements of various crop value chains and processes.

Source Trace has also developed a useful software service called the Carbon Trace, which helps organizations solve the data challenge in carbon farming [31]. Carbon Trace has the unique distinction of being useful for large farms as well as small farm holdings.

With the help of this service, it is possible to unite farmers in order to include them in the sustainability network and passing on the benefits of carbon sequestration down to the smallest contributors. Carbon Trace allows to bring all stakeholders (farmers, inspectors and traders) on one platform and capture verifiable data from the ground at very stage by the combination of ground and satellite data to leave no gaps.

As might be known, sustainable agriculture is closely related to the organic sector, but in essence it is much more. The transition from conventional to sustainable agriculture is not an easy task, as it requires useful technical advice for farmers, investment, charitable donations and stakeholder support (large manufacturing companies, national government and a global initiative).

For example, the largest corporation Syngenta, in its Modern Agriculture Platform (MAP) business model, has established a soil testing service (China) to provide farmers with customized end-to-end planting solutions for precision farming [32]. With the help of MAP, the entire process has been digitized and informatized, from field sampling of soils to the development of online solutions. Soil samples are taken using an automatic vehicle, then an individual QR (quick-response) code is generated for each sample (the data contain the coordinates of the sampling site, farm profile and test results). These data are uploaded to the MAP Soil digital platform database. After that, agronomists and farmers receive a message on client terminals with a reminder to check the test results online. The MAP Soil big data platform contains a

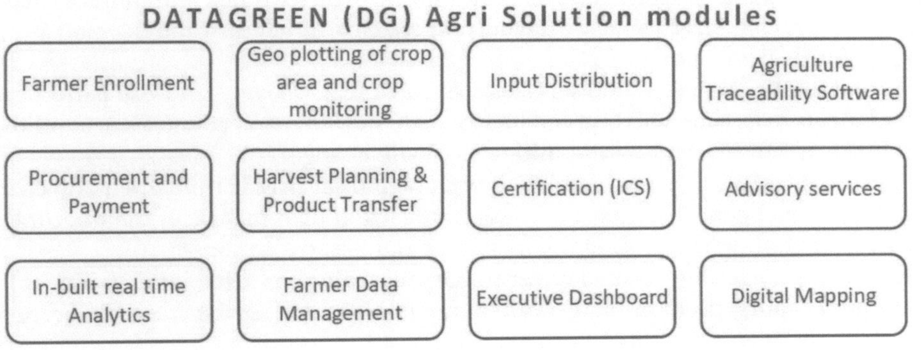

Figure 6.
DG Agri solution modules. Image source: Modified by the authors based on [31].

nationwide soil-type database and a 30x30 m square soil nutrient database. These data are used to develop regional fertilizer packages and recommendations for precision farming. At present, the MAP Soil big data platform has soil data for 2552 counties in China, as well as distribution data maps of more than 200 soil-type subcategories, accounting for almost 100% of China's soil types.

Farmers are both users and creators of big data, and the impact of digital services on farmer behavior is all-encompassing and far-reaching. Agricultural platform digital services not only provide database development, they also encourage farmers to continuously upload their data to help them make sound management decisions. These services shape the specific behavior of farmers in the following aspects:

- rational and optimal distribution of agricultural resources;
- gradual reduction in environmental pollution;
- improvement in the agricultural production system for the rapid development of agricultural economy,
- changing the thinking and consciousness of farmers regarding the need to conduct agriculture in accordance with the concept of its sustainable development.

For example, supported by the European Commission's DG Agriculture and Rural Development, by the EU Space Programme (The Directorate-General for Defense Industry and Space (DG DEFIS)) and by the EU ISA2 Programme (The European Commission's Directorate General for Informatics (DG DIGIT)), the FaST digital service platform will make available capabilities for agriculture, environment and sustainability to European Union (EU) farmers, Member State Paying Agencies, farm advisors and developers of digital solutions [33].

The FaST digital platform helps farmers to improve crop management models, simplify day-to-day management and improve economic efficiency while protecting the environment. Also, FaST facilitates the exchange of information between farmers, as well as between farmers and other stakeholders regarding the experience of growing crops. For the relevant EU institutions, the FaST platform helps to provide environmental monitoring of agricultural land, improve two-way communication with farmers, computerize agriculture, simplify work processes and develop appropriate standards. For policymakers, the FaST platform provides a quick search for agricultural data, which helps to analyze the current state of agriculture and develop a strategy for its development [34].

Access to easy-to-use digital services that track forest cover, land-use patterns and their changes over time will become increasingly important as countries around the world take action to adapt to and mitigate climate change.

The use of satellite images combined with digital services is fundamentally changing how national governments can assess, control and plan the use of their natural resources, including monitoring deforestation and desertification.

Effective policies by national governments regarding the safety and quality of agricultural inputs, products and services can help develop agribusiness by increasing the productivity and profits of farmers.

Thus, digital agricultural platform services make it possible to efficiently collect and disseminate information, compare supply and demand in the markets, and optimize market activities. They also help to facilitate the exchange of knowledge in the field of agriculture, which significantly increases the efficiency of its management.

8. Conclusions

Nowadays, with full confidence, it can be argued that the digitalization of agriculture is not a goal, but a means to ensure its sustainable development. However, this process is rather complicated and slow. It constantly requires the public and private sectors of the economy of each country to adjust the regulatory framework and effective management.

This concerns, first of all, the open data policy. In Europe, since 2003 [35, 36], the practice has been to provide stakeholders with as much data as possible. This practice helps farmers access data for use in the production process. However, there are still not enough valuable data sets published at present. The public sector of national economies can intervene in many areas of open data policy to improve initiatives to provide open data, manage big data and strengthen farmers' rights. These may include measures such as increasing public investment in open database development, improving data ownership and integrity policies, developing sound standards for data processing and use, enforcing data protection and privacy policies, enacting competition laws and securing public-private partnerships to that agricultural data be a public good, not a private good.

At the same time, the development of governance mechanisms that build user confidence and trust in digital agricultural platforms will increase the demand for digital services for the agricultural sector and the food system.

Undeniable advantages are high speed of data processing and efficiency in the formation of initial indicators for an unlimitedly wide set of grouping characteristics and factorial criteria, process of analysis and the optimization of production and communication processes carried out on its basis.

The integration of the control function of data verification at the stage of their receipt, and not after the end of processing, allows to improve the quality of management decisions, as well as limiting the access of a person as a negative factor and reducing the likely negative impact.

The analytical function can be implemented at each stage of the process through a deep analysis of the totality of the array of information that naturally develops in the process of continuous operation of the enterprise.

World experience shows that new technologies are the driver of socioeconomic development.

The technology of risk-free agriculture is a striking example of a new innovative technology that has been widely developed [37]. The usage of this technology in the production of agricultural products allows you to obtain a stable crop quality, efficient use of water, a controlled plant factory environment, and allows you to achieve a level of ultra-high efficiency with minimal land use.

Today, digital technologies are especially important for sustainable agricultural development, which are very effective for the circular economy. Circular economy is also an industrial system that is restorative or regenerative by intention and design. It replaces the "end-of-life" concept with restoration, shifts toward the use of renewable energy, eliminates the use of toxic chemicals, which impair reuse, and aims for the elimination of waste through the superior design of materials, products, systems and, to develop within this, business models [38].

One of the significant steps toward the practical construction of a circular economy is the European Green Deal (EGD) initiative of the EU countries. In accordance with the EGD, the goal is to make the EU climate carbon neutral by 2050 [39]. At the heart of this EU initiative is the goal of transforming the economy for sustainable agricultural development and the transition to a sustainable food system.

Unfortunately, corruption weakens global and national institutions of sustainable development, which creates ineffectiveness of strategic achievements and people's confidence in acquiring positive changes, which in turn leads to the transfer of strong players and resources to other projects. "Corruption drains more than 5 per cent of the global GDP," said Lachezara Stoeva. "Of the approximately $13 trillion in global public spending, up to 25 per cent is lost to corruption." That translates into at least $3 trillion for public spending. Under the theme, Unleashing the transformative power of Sustainable Development Goal (SDG) 16: Improving governance and reducing corruption, the special meeting aimed at identifying concrete solutions to promote anti-corruption practices at all levels [40].

Evidence from 22 OECD (Organization for Economic Cooperation and Development) countries suggests that the negative impact of corruption on the Total Factor Productivity growth over a 20-year period is due to corruption undermining technological change and companies' incentives to build up entrepreneurial skills, invest in innovation, research and development, which are crucial ingredients for sustainable growth (Salinas-Jiménez and Salinas-Jiménez, 2007 [41].

Perspective for further research: due to the persistent trend of reducing the number of agricultural workers and the increase in the number of final consumers of food, it is necessary to adapt digital solutions primarily for food-critical agricultural products, the production of which will become problematic. Also, digital solutions will help reduce the risks of climate and environmental aspects, which urgently require workers who can manage data using platforms. We anticipate that in the next 10 years there may be food shortages where human participation is most needed. The labor shortage issue in agricultural sector, artificial intelligence and the preferences of the young generation will only increase this trend of food safety risks in the future.

The agricultural platform must control all the resources included in agricultural production, as well as the full production chain ending with the end consumer, the threats that bring us closer to a global catastrophe and neutralize their impact on the rhythm, sufficiency, balance and sustainability of the natural environment. This is a complex accounting and analytical task—to collect information and communication links of different industries and regions; however, with the help of modern digital capabilities, this will be feasible in the near future.

Acknowledgements

The corresponding author ensures that all contributing coauthors and no uninvolved persons are included in the author list. The corresponding author also verifies that all coauthors have approved the final version of the article and have agreed to its submission for publication. The authors are responsible for the content of the article and for the fact of its publication.

Author details

Viktor Zamlynskyi[1]*, Tetyana Shabatura[2], Olga Zamlynska[2] and Evgeniya Borysevych[1]

1 State University of Intelligent Technologies and Communications, Ukraine

2 Odesa State Agrarian University, Ukraine

*Address all correspondence to: zam.agrariy@gmail.com

References

[1] World Government Summit. 2018. Available from: https://www.worldgovernmentsummit.org/observer/reports/2018#

[2] UN DESA. 2021. Available from: https://www.un.org/development/desa/dspd/world-social-report/2021-2.html

[3] TechRepublic. 2018. Available from: https://www.techrepublic.com/resource-library/research/digital-transformation-research-report-2018-strategy-returns-on-investment-and-challenges/

[4] United Nations Global Compact. 2017. Available from: https://unglobalcompact.org/library/5431

[5] Robotics Business Review. 2019. Available from: https://www.roboticsbusinessreview.com/health-medical/5-surgical-robots-2019/

[6] OECD. 2018b. Available from: https://data.oecd.org/

[7] The World Bank Annual Report. 2019. Available from: https://documents.worldbank.org/en/publication/documents-reports/documentdetail/156691570147766895/the-world-bank-annual-report-2019-ending-poverty-investing-in-opportunity

[8] Cisco. Available from: https://www.cisco.com/c/en/us/solutions/data-center-virtualization/what-is-a-data-center.html electronic resource [date of access 18/03/2023]

[9] National Institute of Standards and Technology. NIST Definition of Cloud Computing v15, release date 2/07/2011. Available from: https://csrc.nist.gov/publications/sp#800-145

[10] IaaS vs. PaaS vs. SaaS - IBM. Available from: https://www.ibm.com/topics/iaas-paas-saas electronic resource [date of access 02/03/2023]

[11] Microsoft. Available from: https://www.microsoft.com, electronic resource [date of access 2/02/2023]

[12] Serra Parajes Javier, Márquez AC, Rosique AS. Criticality analysis for optimising OPEX cost lifecycle. IFAC-PapersOnLine. 2016;**49**(28):7-12. Available from: https://www.sciencedirect.com/science/article/pii/S2405896316324260

[13] Cloud Service Models. Available from: https://www.doi.gov/cloud/serviceelectronic resource [date of access 05/03/2023]

[14] Learn About FaaS, a Cloud Computing Service Model. Available from: https://www.intel.com/content/www/us/en/cloud-computing/faas.html electronic resource [date of access 15/02/2023]

[15] Communication from the commission to the European parliament, the council, the European economic and social committee and the committee of the regions. Online Platforms and the Digital Single Market. Opportunities and Challenges for Europe //European commission. 2016. Available from: https://eur-lex.europa.eu/legal-content/EN/TXT/?uri=CELEX%3A52016DC0288

[16] Bourreau M, Valletti T. Enabling digital financial inclusion through improvements in competition and interoperability: What works and what Doesn't? In: CGD Policy Paper 065. Washington DC: Center for Global Development; June 16, 2015. Available

from: https://www.researchgate.net/publication/284124402_Enabling_Digital_Financial_Inclusion_through_Improvements_in_Competition_and_Interoperability_What_Works_and_What_Doesn't

[17] Evans P, Gawer A. The rise of the platform Enterprise: A global survey. The Center for Global Enterprise. Surrey Business School Report. 2016:9. Available from: https://openresearch.surrey.ac.uk/esploro/outputs/99516671002346

[18] Hagiu A, Wright J. Multi-sided platforms. In: Harvard Business School Working Paper. No 15-037 (March 16). USA: Harvard Business School; 2015. Available from: https://www.hbs.edu/ris/Publication%20Files/15-037_cb5afe51-6150-4be9-ace2-39c6a8ace6d4.pdf

[19] Cropwise. Available from: https://www.cropwise.com/#where-are-we, electronic resource [date of access 12/03/2023]

[20] FAO. Available from: https://www.fao.org/digital-agriculture/digital-portfolio/en/ electronic resource [date of access 02/04/2023]

[21] Digital Agriculture Platform Blueprints. January 2021. Available from: https://www.mercycorpsagrifin.org/2021/01/28/introducing-the-digital-agriculture-platform-blueprint-series-with-giz-dalberg/

[22] Qin T, Wang L, Zhou Y, Guo L, Jiang G, Zhang L. Digital technology-and-services-driven sustainable transformation of agriculture: Cases of China and the EU. Agriculture. 2022;**12**:297. Available from: https://www.mdpi.com/2077-0472/12/2/297

[23] Wysel M, Baker D, Billingsley W. Data sharing platforms: How value is created from agricultural data. Agricultural Systems, October 2021, volume 193,103241. Available from: https://www.sciencedirect.com/science/article/abs/pii/S0308521X21001943?via%3Dihub

[24] Amazon Web Services. Available from: https://aws.amazon.com electronic resource [date of access 22/12/2022]

[25] Zhai Z, Martínez JF, Beltran V, Martínez NL. Decision support systems for agriculture 4.0: Survey and challenges. Computers and Electronics in Agriculture. 2020;**170**:105256. Available from: https://www.sciencedirect.com/science/article/pii/S0168169919316497?via%3Dihub

[26] Athey S, Catalini C, Tucker C. The Digital Privacy Paradox: Small Money, Small Costs, Small Talk; Working Paper No. 23488. Cambridge, MA, USA: National Bureau of Economic Research; 2017. Available from: https://www.nber.org/system/files/working_papers/w23488/w23488.pdf

[27] Farmable. Available from: https://farmable.tech/pricing/, electronic resource, date of access 8/04/2023

[28] Ansi-Eia-Tia-942-2005 Telecommunications Infrastructure Standard for Data Centers, January 2005. Available from: https://www.academia.edu/7700352/Ansi_Eia_Tia_942_2005_Telecommunications_Infrastructure_Standard_For_Data_Centers

[29] Wolfert S, Ge L, Verdouw C, Bogaardt M-J. Big data in smart farming – A review. Agricultural Systems. 2017;**153**:69-80. Available from: https://www.sciencedirect.com/science/article/pii/S0308521X16303754#f0025

[30] Barman A, Saha P, Patel S, Bera A. Crop diversification an effective strategy for sustainable agriculture development.

Published: April 9th, 2022. Available from: https://www.intechopen.com/chapters/81179

[31] SourceTrace. Available from: https://www.sourcetrace.com/agriculture-solutions/ electronic resource [date of access 28/03/2023]

[32] MAP. Green Development Report. 2021. p. 25. Available from: https://www.researchgate.net/publication/368831333_MAP_2021_Green_Development_Report_Syngenta_Group_China

[33] EU Space Data for Sustainable Farming. Available from: https://fastplatform.eu/ electronic resource [date of access 02/02/2023]

[34] Pradhan RP, Arvin MB, Nair M, Bennett SE. Sustainable economic growth in the European Union: The role of ICT, venture capital, and innovation. Review of Financial Economics. 2019;**38**:34-62. Available from: https://onlinelibrary.wiley.com/doi/10.1002/rfe.1064

[35] Recent EU legislation for research access to confidential data: implementation and implications: paper/submitted by Eurostat. Available from: https://digitallibrary.un.org/record/495972 electronic resource [date of access 20/02/2023]

[36] Directive 2003/4/EC of the European Parliament and of the Council on public access to environmental information and repealing Council Directive 90/313/EEC. Available from: https://eur-lex.europa.eu/legal-content/EN/TXT/?uri=celex%3A32003L0004

[37] Farminova. The future of agriculture. Available from: https://www.farminova.com/ electronic resource [date of access 14/06/2023]

[38] Özçatalbaş O. An Evaluation of the Transition from Linear Economy to Circular Economy. Published: January 17th, 2023. Available from: https://www.intechopen.com/chapters/84351#tab1

[39] EU. Policy Document: The European Green Deal. Brussels: European Environment Information and Observation Network (Eionet); 2019. Available from: https://www.eea.europa.eu/policy-documents/com-2019-640-final

[40] Available from: https://news.un.org/en/story/2023/05/1136282

[41] del Mar Salinas-Jiménez M, Salinas-Jiménez J. Corruption, efficiency and productivity in OECD countries. Journal of Policy Modeling. 2007;**29**(6):903-915, ISSN 0161-8938. DOI: 10.1016/j.jpolmod.2007.07.002

Section 2

Strategies and Cases

Chapter 2

Fresh Chili Agribusiness: Opportunities and Problems in Indonesia

Amos Lukas, Agustinus N. Kairupan, Agung Hendriadi, Arief Arianto, Lamhot Parulian Manalu, Lanjar Sumarno, Joni Munarso, Mulyana Hadipernata, Huda M. Elmatsani, Bonnie O. Benyamin, Akhmad Junaidi, Mochammad Jusuf Djafar, Roosganda Elizabeth, Sahlan, Nasruddin, Puji Astuti, Subandrio, Heryoki Yohanes, Ermi E. Koeslulat, Eko Bhakti Susetyo, Suharto Ngudiwaluyo, Abdul Halik, Wahyu Purwanto, Guntur Haryanto, Sitti Ramlah, Noverina Sjafrina, Agus Budiyanto, Sari Intan Kailaku, Rienoviar, Alvi Yani, Nenie Yustiningsih, Himawan Adinegoro, Henky Henanto, Payung Layuk, Meivie Lintang, Gabriel H. Joseph, Derek Polakitan, Heri Wahyudianto, Joko Saptohadi, Kusumawati Dewi Budiarti, Taufik Hidayat, Josep Ginting, Amsal Rasyid and August Polakitan

Abstract

The National Socioeconomic Survey (SUSENAS) conducted in Indonesia in September 2021 found that the average consumption of red chili per month was 0.15 kilograms (kg) per capita per month. The average consumption of fresh chili per month is 40.90 thousand tons, and the cumulative total reached 490.83 thousand tons in 2021. Uneven chili production across time and region makes prices fluctuate, which affects inflation by 0.01–0.07%. Another problem is the imbalance of supply and demand between time and region, which impacts farmers' welfare. Setting planting time and location and improving distribution can solve these problems. The application of technology that can extend the life of fresh chilies for one month is a solution for chili distribution from farmers to areas with high demand. One-wave roasting and drying technology can extend chilies' freshness for six months. By producing chilies that have a shelf life of more than three months, it is possible to store them in warehouses using the warehouse receipt system. The application of the warehouse receipt system to chili commodities is also an alternative to solving postharvest problems. The distribution and application of technology that can extend the life of chili can increase its economic value and make chili not a commodity that contributes to Indonesian inflation.

Keywords: chili consumption, opportunities, agribusiness, distribution, application of technology

1. Introduction

Fresh chili has been designated as one of the main commodities, so it has become one of the focuses of programs and activities in agricultural development. Policies and programs for the development of fresh chili have been carried out to increase production and require the problem of price fluctuations and increased availability [1]. One of the Horticultural Crops commodities that are continually needed by the community of Indonesia is red chili. Some areas in Indonesia use red chilies as one of the essential spices because chili has a hot taste [2]. The output must be raised using a variety of red chilies, and to meet the demand for red chilies, expenses must be decreased.

According to data from the Indonesian Central Bureau of Statistics (BPS), red chili is one of the top five vegetable crops in terms of production during the last five years, omitting shallots, potatoes, cabbage, and chilies. The national production of red chili reached 1.36 million tons in 2021. West Java, North Sumatra, and Central Java had the highest total of red chili production in 2021, with 343.07 thousand tons, 210.22 thousand tons, and 169.28 thousand tons, respectively. Household consumption of red chili increased by 9.94% in 2021, reaching 490.83 thousand tons. Furthermore, market operations hit 8.23% of red chili traders in 2021, while natural catastrophes impacted 50.85% of them the previous year.

Fresh red chili production tends to increase from year to year from 2012 to 2022. **Figure 1** shows fresh red chili production from 2012 to 2022.

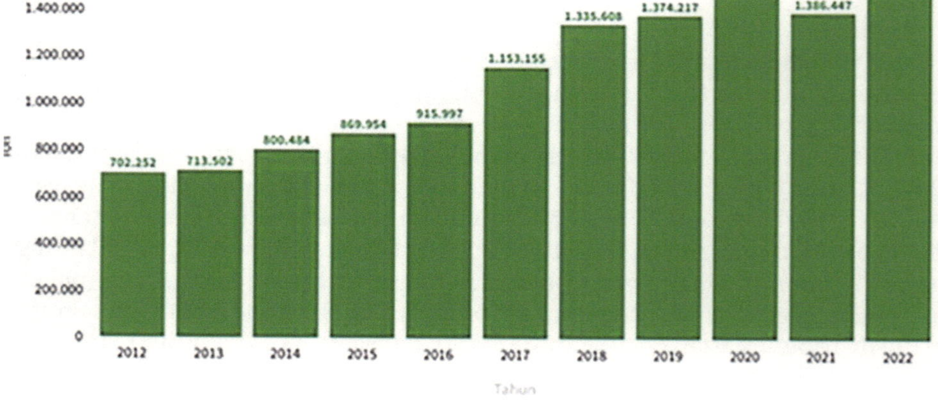

Figure 1.
Fresh red chili production 2012–2022 [3].

Based on **Figure 1**, production of fresh red chili in 2012 amounted to 702.25 thousand tonnes in 2012 increased to 713.5 thousand tonnes in 2013, 800.48 thousand tonnes in 2014, 869.95 thousand tonnes in 2015, and 916 thousand tons in year 2016. Fresh red chili production continued to increase beyond 1 million tons in 2017, 1.15 million tons increasing to 1.34 million tons in 2018, increasing to 1.37 million tons in 2019, and increasing again 1.51 million tons in year 2020.

Fresh red chili production experienced a decline in 2021 compared to 2020 to 1.39 million. The covid-19 epidemic is largely to blame for this. The decline in cayenne pepper production in 2021 is the first time in the last decade. From 2011 to 2020, it is known that cayenne pepper production has continued to increase every year.

The production of fresh red chilies has again increased to 1.55 million tons in 2022, exceeded the production of fresh red chilies in 2020. Compared to 2021, the production of fresh red chilies in 2022 has increased by 11.5% compared to 2021. The increase in fresh red chili production from year to year for the last 10 years shows that fresh red chili is a promising product in the future.

There is an adage that Indonesians cannot live without chili sauce. Various foods taste less delicious if not served with chili sauce. In fact, some people are willing to eat before the chili sauce is served. Due to people's love for chili sauce, the demand for cayenne pepper as one of the raw materials in Indonesia is quite high. It also encourages the large production of cayenne pepper in the country in last 10 years.

Seeing the trend, cayenne pepper production has tended to increase in the last decade. Indonesia's cayenne pepper production touched its highest level at 2022. Meanwhile, East Java is the province with the largest cayenne pepper production in Indonesia, 578,883 tons. This amount contributes 41.75% to the national cayenne pepper production. Central Java is second with cayenne pepper production of 179,287 tons or 1293%. Meanwhile, West Java produced 137,456 tons of cayenne pepper, or 9.91%. Some areas that are production centers of cayenne pepper in East Java province include Malang, Blitar, and Nganjuk districts [4, 5].

Red chili is one of the vegetable commodities most consumed by Indonesian people. This high level of consumption is inseparable from Indonesian culinary culture, which uses red chilies as a basic spice or food flavoring. The National Socioeconomic Survey (SUSENAS) conducted in Indonesia in September 2021 found that the average consumption of red chili per month was 0.15 kilograms (kg) per capita per month. **Figure 2** shows the consumption of red chilies for the last five years, from 2017 to 2021.

According to **Figure 2**, red chili consumption has declined from 479.65 thousand tons in 2017 to 469.15 thousand tons in 2018. The consumption of red chilies fell again in 2019 to 406.77 thousand tons. Furthermore, red chili consumption climbed to 446.46 tons in 2020. However, red chili consumption in 2020 is still lower than the maximum level in 2017. Red chili consumption is expected to reach 490.83 tons in 2021.

The average consumption of fresh chili per month is 40.9025 thousand tons, and the cumulative total reached 490.83 thousand tons in 2021. This number increased by 9.94% from consumption in 2020 and is the highest consumption in the last five years. The province with the highest consumption of red chilies in 2021 is West Sumatra, which is 0.59 kg/capita/month. The food of the people in the Mining Realm almost all use red chilies as a flavor enhancer. The next largest consumption comes from Bengkulu, which is 0.58 kg/capita/month, Jambi 0.46 kg/capita/month, and Riau 0.37 kg/capita/month.

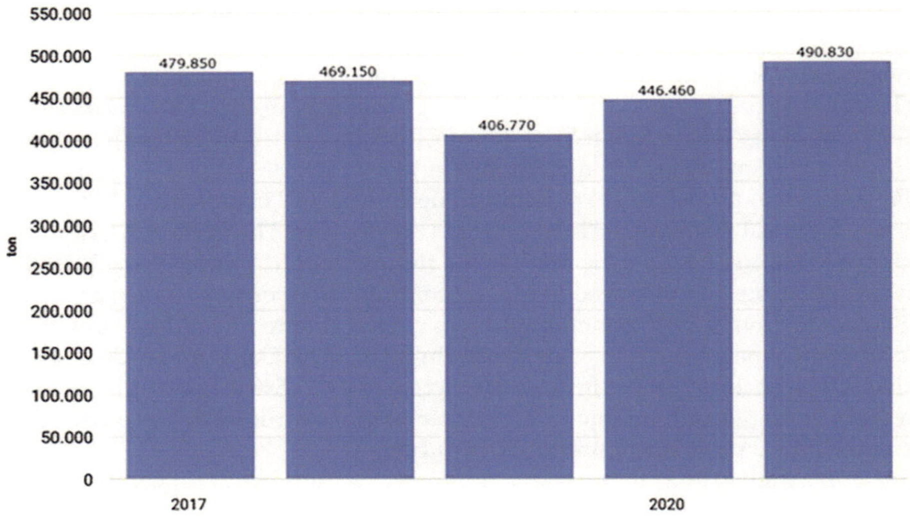

Figure 2.
Consumption of red chilies 2017–2021.

The volume of domestic demand makes chili a promising commodity. Chili request high demand for cooking spices, and the food and drug sector is profit potential. Not surprisingly, chili is a Horticultural commodity that experienced the largest price swings in Indonesia [6].

Fresh chili is a commodity that has the highest price fluctuation compared to other horticultural products. Sometimes the price of fresh red chili can be high at one time, then drop at a certain time. Uneven chili production across time and region makes prices fluctuate, which affects inflation by 0.01–0.07%.

Until now, the government has not succeeded in reducing the high fluctuations in chilies. Chili is a food that can only be stored for a short time. Thus, the condition of chili stocks is very influential on the weather and harvest season. Chili price fluctuations can be suppressed if there is a buffer stock for chili commodities. This means that some of the harvested chilies will be processed first and stored for a long time. However, the buffer stock strategy for chili is difficult to implement because Indonesians prefer to eat fresh chilies. In addition, storing chilies to keep them fresh is still very expensive. Thus, a stock solution for fresh chilies cannot be feasible now. For chili, it is more manageable to spread production, both between regions and between regions over time.

Red chili development policies and programs have been carried out so far, increasing production, underdelivering the problem of price fluctuations, and increasing around-the-clock availability. Generally, farmers in chili production areas and centers red are experienced and able to apply appropriate cultivation technology recommendations, even though business management still encounters obstacles, such as setting production patterns, setting planting schedules, and synchronizing production patterns production between regions and production centers. Aspects of the use of production technology may is said to have been successful. It is just that business actors still need to improve in handling postharvest and product processing, so the availability of red chili cannot always be fulfilled.

Most of the ages in large chili farming families are in the productive age. Productive age is support in family life related to welfare. The more productive family members, the more family members work to meet their needs in achieving a level of welfare. In chili agribusiness, many family members, and dependents have >5 family members/responsible [5].

In the context of chili prices, the situation involves many small-scale farmers with limited land and production capacity. These farmers depend on intermediaries or large traders to sell their chili harvests in the market. Because of this dependence, an imbalance in bargaining power arises, favoring the intermediaries, who control the supply of chili produce from numerous small-scale farmers and determine the selling price.

Due to their reliance on intermediaries and the lack of direct access to better markets, small-scale farmers often receive low selling prices for their chilies, leading to reduced profitability. In contrast, intermediaries take advantage of this situation to gain excessive profits by setting higher selling prices for end consumers compared to what they pay to farmers. This complex system poses challenges for small farmers, impacting their income and market opportunities, while intermediaries benefit significantly.

As a result, during the red chili harvest, the stock becomes abundant and causes the chili price to drop to its lowest point. However, after the harvest period is over, due to the short shelf life of fresh red chili products, the availability of fresh red chili products on the market becomes scarce. It ultimately causes the price of fresh red chili to soar.

The handling of red chili results is generally done at the farmer level, and is restricted to simple cleaning, sorting, drying, and packing of fresh chili; many do not even complete this stage at all, namely the result. Traders/middlemen sell the harvest immediately on the field and transport it to the truck. Furthermore, the method of handling during packaging and Transportation is still crude and less practical (heaped up, compacted, and without enough aeration). As a result, rate damage and yield losses (postharvest losses) are still significant and can even reach 50%. These issues and circumstances frequently arise during the primary harvest, resulting in a production buildup and a consequent drop in pricing. This harms farmers' and business operators' ability to secure production and revenues.

Stepping up the use of postharvest handling technology and processing of chili products, such as red cayenne pepper, which is done through excavation and the introduction of appropriate technology, guidance, and technology assistance, as well as the provision of postharvest facilities are one effort and strategy is made to address this problem. A small amount of study is still being done on handling and processing chili products after harvest. However, the focus is largely on areas of pure research (pure science and technology). Therefore, the field of applied research needs to be developed and highlighted for it to be applied.

Drying and roasting technology will reduce the red chili's volume and weight, extend its shelf life, and increase its economic value, facilitating transportation [7]. However, so far, research emphasizing the application of appropriate technology still needs to be improved. Therefore, a breakthrough in postharvest processing and technology research is called for further investigation. Chili can easily solve field problems and then disseminate them to farmers and business actors.

2. Indonesia in global chili pepper trade, production, and consumption

The year 2018, Indonesia was a major player in worldwide hot pepper trade, production, and consumption. As the world's second-largest chili producer, Indonesia contributed considerably to the entire chili peppers supply in the international market, producing 88,000 tons of chili peppers and demonstrating its solid position as a key global producer (**Figures 3–5**) [3].

Additionally, Indonesia actively participated in the hot pepper export sector, ranking 3rd globally in terms of hot pepper exports. With 36,000 tons of hot peppers exported (**Table 1**), the country demonstrated its crucial role in supplying hot peppers to other nations and contributing to the global hot pepper trade. The main export destinations of Indonesian chili in 2021 were Saudi Arabia, Nigeria, and Taiwan, contributing 37.20% (equivalent to USD 8.35 million), 14.16% (equivalent to USD 3.18 million), and 7.33% (equivalent to USD 1.65 million), respectively. This was followed by Malaysia at 5.48% (equivalent to USD 1.23 million). The combined contribution of these top five countries reached 69.03% of the total value of Indonesian chili exports.

Moreover, Indonesia features among the top consuming countries, registering at 5th place in chili consumption. Indonesia is included in the group of countries with a consumption volume of 242,000 tons, highlighting the significant consumption of chilies.

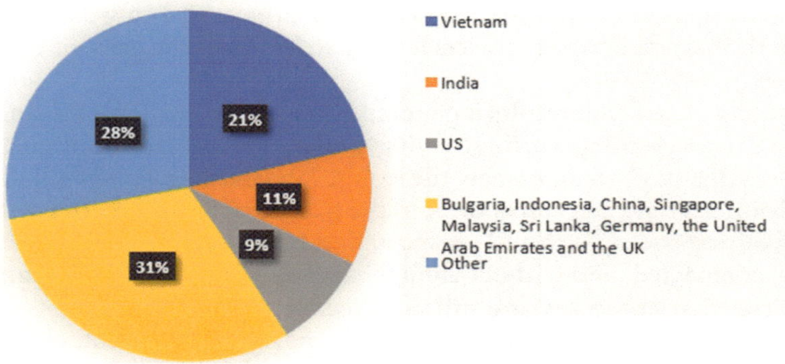

Figure 3.
World chili pepper consumption.

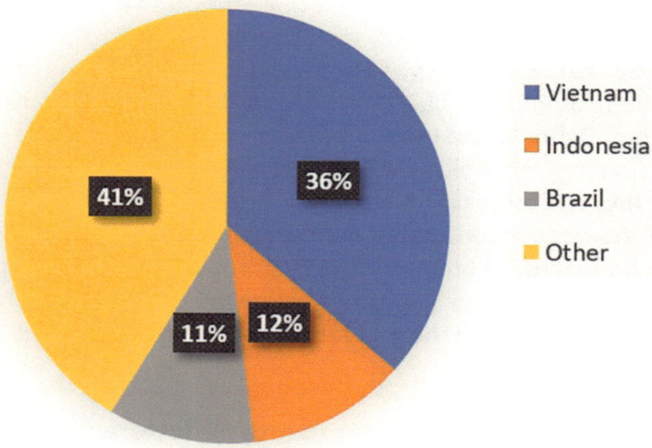

Figure 4.
World chili pepper production.

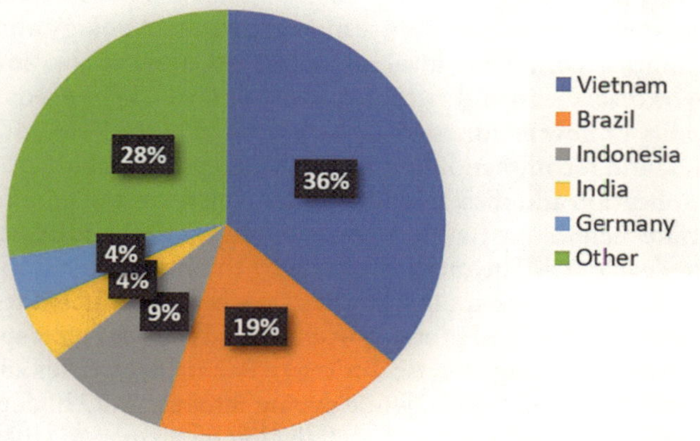

Figure 5.
World chili pepper export.

Export	Production	Consumption
• Vietnam (142,000) • Brazil (73,000) • Indonesia (36,000) • India (17,000) • Germany (16,000)	• Vietnam (273,000) • Indonesia (88,000) • Brazil (80,000)	• Vietnam (166,000) • India (86,000) • U.S. (68,000) • Bulgaria, Indonesia, China, Singapore, Malaysia, Sri Lanka, Germany, the United Arab Emirates, and the UK (242,000)

Table 1.
World chili pepper export, production, and consumption in 2018, tons.

3. Framework and formulation of the problem

The data demonstrate that growers and producers of chili have a strong production or cultivation technical foundation. Just a few people are still adept at using postharvest handling techniques to lengthen the shelf life of chili products. This practice results in many damaged and rotten chilies that cannot be stored for an extended period. As a result, farmers gain little profit and additional value, and their products are usually less competitive. Another reality is that there are irregularities in the production and supply of chili, including high demand for fresh chili among customers and an abundance of production during specific seasons (particularly the dry season). This circumstance results in extreme price changes, which ultimately produce inflation.

Field observations and preliminary research revealed that despite the government's provision of numerous facilities and assistance (postharvest wards, harvest baskets, blowers, dryers, flour, packaging machines, etc.), some aspects of handling postharvest still need to be improved. This problem was significantly linked to policy, planning, practice capital, yield marketing management, and institutional help, as well as farmers' low/lack of knowledge and technology.

Implementing handling technologies postharvest to create dry chilies and continue the processing into chili powder or other goods is an effort that needs to be made to increase chili's added value and competitiveness. Technology for postharvest handling and Chile processing currently exists and has even been extensively produced. However, the reality is that the use of suggested technology and postharvest technology in chilies at the farmer level is still limited, and the creation of norms and SOPs has yet to be discovered and put into practice there. There needs to be a match between the reality of how technology is being applied in the field and the conclusions, guidelines, and recommendations of technology research.

Make the application and dissemination among farmers and commercial actors easier, appropriate technology (applicative technology) for handling chili after harvest must be developed. The method of drying this chili still requires a lot of time, despite the fact that numerous applied studies have been conducted to look for technology that makes handling and processing chili goods easier (fruit splitting, balancing process, filtering, grinding, etc. According to Bahar [8], it takes 28–38 h to bake food to a moisture content of 9.47%, while drying it takes 33–77 h, depending on the quantity and weather. The efficiency of chili drying by farmers is still too high low, which is about 10% (because they do not follow the SOP, while the research results are carried out by Bahar [8] ranged from 29 to 21%. Therefore, it is necessary to look for technology to speed up the drying process.

In addition to using red chili drying technique to extend the life of red chili product, roasting technique using Far-Infrared Radiation are also carried out. IR radiation is energy in the form of electromagnetic wave and lies in the wavelength range between 0.78 and 1000 μm. It is more rapid in heat transfer than convection and conduction mechanism. IR radiation has received considerable attention lately because of its advantages in shortening drying time, high energy transfer rate, energy saving, and superior product quality compare to conventional heated air drying FIR wavelength lies in the wavelength range between 4 and 1000 μm and the FIR heat application can be classified into four major categories as baking, drying, thawing, and pasteurization [9].

Based on the above framework, the problem can be formulated as follows:

1. Fresh red cayenne pepper does not have a limited shelf life, there will be a lot of unsold chilies that will ultimately rot or incorrect postharvest treatment, which will be negative for farmers and destabilize prices if there is an excessive output.

2. After the harvest period, especially during the rainy season, there is a scarcity of red cayenne pepper on the market due to low production or difficulty in distribution and low availability of red chili, so the price of chili increases high and is detrimental to consumers.

3. One of the keys to handling this problem is the application of technology postharvest and product processing through drying and roasting techniques of fresh red chili products, but knowledge, discovery, and application of efficient, appropriate technology for postharvest handling and processing of fresh red chilies into dried chilies and powdered chilies are still limited.

4. Overview of fresh chili

The red chili plant (*Capsicum annum L.*) is a shrub that develops and is a member of the Solanaceae family of plants. Red chili containing annual or short-lived plants hails from the American continent to be precise Peru, then spreads to the Americas, Europe, and Asia including Indonesia [2].

Various chilies, which are generally red chilies (*Capsicum annum L.*) and red cayenne pepper (*Capsicum frutescens*), are the main horticultural commodities which is a herbaceous plant with a spicy fruit taste because of the capsaicin content. Chili includes the active chemicals capsaicin and dihydrocapsaicin, which give it a distinct spicy flavors. Other content contained in chili is carotenoids, fats, proteins, and vitamins A and C. Chilies will ripen physiologically at 70–75 HST and in the highlands after 4–5 months old. The feature is that some of the fruit is red. The first harvest of chili is determined by several factors' environment, varieties, and cultivation methods. Harvesting can be done by picking, with a frequency of once every 3–4 days, and can be harvested up to 7–8 months old.

Chili comprises numerous types, and the most generally recognized is chili big red, curly chilies, red cayenne peppers, and green chilies. Red chili consists of big chili and curled chili. Chili has a value high economy and is much needed by all levels of society as flavoring and food seasoning. Red chilies can be marketed in numerous forms, such as young/green chilies, old fruit, fresh fruit, industrial materials (milled, dried, flour), processed, and industrial products. Fresh chiles spoil quickly; they can only be stored for 2–3 days at room temperature; after that, they will decline in quality and wilting. If the postharvest management process is conducted, the good ones will last more than five days. The postharvest handling technique for fresh chili begins with the right harvesting (picking) process, sorting and processing grading, and good storage methods [10].

5. Harvest and postharvest chili

Implementing Good Postharvest Handling (Good Handling Practices = GHP) will produce quality products ready to enter the modern market, reduce yield loss, maintain quality, extend life storage, and produce safe products for consumption. The application of GHP has become imperative to meet consumer demand for quality and safe product consumption and production in an environmentally friendly manner. Permentan Guidelines for Harvesting, Post harvesting, and Management of Horticultural Postharvest Wards No 73/Permentan/OT.140/7/2013, (Good Horticulture Packing House Management) provides detailed implementation of the good postharvest application mandated by Law No. 13 of 2010 concerning Horticulture.

Several initiatives are being implemented in Indonesia to promote value-added product processing in the chili sector. These initiatives include research and development to investigate novel processing technologies, infrastructure development to support processing facilities, and capacity building for farmers and processors through training programs. Market promotion, government incentives, and public-private partnerships are also being utilized to encourage investment and innovation in the chili processing business. To boost the value and marketability of Indonesian chili goods, various drying and processing procedures such as sun drying, air drying, freeze-drying, and processing into chili powder, flakes, sauces, and pastes are being investigated. Implementing quality and safety standards is also critical to ensuring the competitiveness and customer acceptance of value-added chili products on a national and international scale.

One of the keys to successful production is the postharvest management of chilies by farming or business actors, which increases added value and product competitiveness. After-harvest processing of chili includes (1) sorting and grading/classifying, (2) curing, specifically by spreading the harvest in a shaded area or chamber, (3) packing to preserve wounds, facilitate shipping, stop water loss, facilitate special treatment, and provide esthetic value, (4) cold storage at 8–12°C with 90–95% humidity will extend the freshness of chili for up to 8 days and (5) to prevent damage or rot, Transportation to trucks, preferably with a refrigerated box car.

According to Asgar et al. [11], the potential for chili yield loss before reaching customers is very large (20–30%) because chili is a commodity that is readily damaged [11]. On the other hand, fresh chili is in high demand for domestic use. Therefore, postharvest treatment of fresh red chilies requires knowledge of and expertise in technology to keep them fresh or transform them into a more durable product. Ozonisation technology is one way to maintain the freshness of golden chili cultivars for as long as storage because it is capable of shedding contamination of pesticides, bacteria, and heavy metals attached to fruits and vegetables, so it is safe for consumption. Treatment of 1% ozone concentration and storage at a temperature of 10°C can maintain the color and freshness of chili for 14 days, with products still preferred by consumers.

6. Chili drying

The most common primary technique of food preservation is drying [9]. Chili is dried to manufacture chili powder and to store for lengthy periods of time [9]. Drying chili into dried chilies or powdered chilies is one method of extending the shelf life of chili. Drying is done to lower the water content of the chili to the point where microbial activity is reduced. That cause putrefaction will be stopped. In drying chilies cayenne pepper, pile weight and drying time using a cabinet dryer really influence the quality of chili powder [12].

Chili is a vegetable commodity that is easily damaged. Therefore, there needs to be an effort to maintain its freshness or process it into products that are more durable. One effort can be made by drying and manufacturing into chili powder. The purpose of drying hot peppers is to reduce the water content, shrink the volume, reduce the growth of microorganisms, and reduce enzyme activity. In principle, in the drying process occurs simultaneously heat and mass transfer. In line, for the most part, the method of drying chili commodities can be distinguished from natural drying using sunlight and artificial drying (mechanical drying).

Mechanical drying is done while monitoring the temperature, humidity, and drying speed. Typically, this drying consists of a propulsion system, fans, heating elements, and control mechanisms. There are several different types of mechanical drying, including (1) cabinet/rack type [13], (2) solar dryers with combined energy [14–17], (3) tunnel type dryers [18], and (4) freeze dryers, which involve the processes of freezing and [19, 20].

Drying chilies can lower their volume and weight, increase their shelf life, increase their economic value, and make them easier to transport as a solution to the issue of damage from low storage temperatures and explosive chili production. There are several methods of drying, including: (1) natural drying in the sunlight, although this method makes it difficult to regulate temperature and humidity and results in changes to the finished product's color; (2) artificial drying techniques, including oil-burning tool dryers, Tropical Plants Research Institute and the Indonesian Institute of Sciences solar dryer models, and simple solar dryers. Immediately after drying, begin packaging with plastic bags [7].

The simplest and least expensive drying process is sunlight-based. However, to decrease dependency and weather interruptions, this activity depends on the location, weather, amenities, and supporting structures. Employing intermediary tools such as an oven, microwave, through-flow air dryer, and far infrared lamp is another mechanical method that can be used. The tool's capacity influences the outcome, the drying process, and the temperature. According to preliminary research findings, drying with FIR results in dried chilies with the maximum quantities of capsaicin and a significantly shorter drying time, i.e. 12 min at 60°C.

Dried red chilies are ground into chili powder (flour) by grinding them until smooth, then passing them through an 80-mesh sieve to smooth them out and storing the flour in a clean bottle or plastic container. Chili powder can be kept at low temperatures of 5–10°C or at room temperature of 28–31°C. This chili powder can be used immediately as a seasoning [7].

The efficiency of drying chili using different technologies (sunlight, oven, and microwave) did not significantly affect the drying process; the efficiency of drying ranged between 20.39% for curly red chilies and 20.49% for big red chilies. In addition, there was no discernible difference in the drying process efficiency between different types of chilies or between whole and Halved Chilies. According to a review of the product's quality and functionality, the drying and production of the chili powder allowed it to remain effective and consumer-acceptable after eight weeks of storage [8]. This further extended the product's shelf life.

The length of the drying process is frequently encountered in the postharvest handling of chilies because after the balancing process (immersion in hot water or heating with steam), the water content of the chili will increase, in addition to the chili itself having a high-water content [21]. This technique will cause drying to take longer, requiring much work and energy. For this reason, extra treatment is carried out by pressing. Suppose the compression results do not significantly influence the settlement quality of red cayenne pepper. In that case, this will also bring benefits and advantages to speed up the drying process.

The first thing to do is add pressing (pressing) in a series of postharvest handling activities of red chili to speed the reduction/decrease in water content and hasten the drying process. Pressing is done with a hydraulic press, followed by guiding, drying, and postharvest processing as usual; the results are dried red chilies and red chili powder. **Table 2** shows the average results of observations with and without compression treatment during the storage period for red chili products.

The data analysis results by t-test on the quality of dry red chili and red chili pepper powder after adding compression and without compression in postharvest handling, with observations during storage of almost the same pattern. The results of this data analysis can be explained as follows:

1. The water content in pressing significantly differs from without pressing; water content with lower pressing indicates better condition. Referring to the recommended water content for storing dried chilies (SNI Chili 4480: 2016 is 12%, while UNECE Standard 2012 is 13.5%) then the average water content with the pressing process meets these standards, while without pressing is seen that only dry cayenne pepper that meets or is close to the standard. From the results of observations during the storage process, it can be said that there is pressing can

Number	Parameter	With compression	Without compression	T-test
1	Water (%)	12.2	13.35	Significant
2	Rot	1.00	1.00	Not significant
3	Aroma	2.46	2.52	Significant
4	Color	2.00	2.12	Significant
5	Taste	2.79	2.73	Significant

Table 2.
Average results of observations with and without compression treatment.

significantly reduce the water content in dried red bird's eye chilies and powdered red cayenne pepper, in addition to the water content conditions of red cayenne pepper dry is better (meets standards/recommendations) compared to water content powdered cayenne pepper.

2. Both with and without the addition of compression treatment, the level of spoilage on dry red cayenne pepper and cayenne pepper powder throughout the storage process was similar, and neither showed rot (nearly all without Mold growth). This issue is related to the low water content and high capsaicin concentration of chilies, making them an unfavorable medium for bacteria.

3. For dry and powdered red bird's eye chilies, the results of the organoleptic tests (aroma, color, and taste) show significantly different values with pressing and without pressing the therapy with pressing produced much superior organ emetic test results than the treatment without compression. The presence of pressing treatment does not appear to affect the organoleptic quality of dried red bird's eye chilies or powdered red bird's eye chilies, even when, with this procedure, quality can be preserved while being stored.

Through weekly inspections of quality parameter data (up until week ten), the accuracy of the dry red cayenne pepper was investigated. The analysis involved comparing the quality conditions in the test week to the original state (zero weeks) and comparing the quality circumstances to the parameters of gradual observation. **Table 3** summarizes the findings from evaluating the dried red cayenne pepper's quality throughout storage using pressing and no-pressing methods.

It may be described as follows based on the data analysis results for dried red chilies provided in **Table 3**:

1. Based on the parameters observed (water content, aroma, color, and taste), it was shown that during the 4 weeks of observation (1 month), the condition of dried red chilies had not shown any difference (still the same as the initial conditions of observation).

2. During storage until the tenth week, all quality parameters show a downward trend (except for the level of decay). This shows that the rates of the theoretical superiority of dried red cayenne pepper continue to decrease over time storage. Until the 10th week, the water content becomes 13.05%; this condition is still quite good and still meets and is close to the recommended storage of the

Numbers	Week	Observation parameters (average)			
		Water	Aroma	Color	Taste
1	Beginning (0)	10.28	1.00	1.00	1.00
2	1	11.05[aa]	1.00[aa]	1.00[aa]	2.00[aa]
3	2	10.23[aa]	1.33[aa]	1.67[aa]	2.33[aa]
4	3	10.71[aa]	2.00[aa]	2.00[aa]	2.66[aa]
5	4	10.41[aa]	2.30[aa]	2.33[aa]	2.00[aa]
6	5	11.16[ab]	3.33[aa]	2.00[aa]	3.67[ab]
7	6	12.15[ab]	3.67[ab]	3.33[ab]	3.67[ab]
8	7	13.06[ab]	3.00[ab]	2.00[ab]	3.00[ab]
9	8	15.22[ab]	3.16[ab]	2.83[ab]	3.33[ab]
10	9	13.16[ab]	2.67[ab]	3.00[ab]	3.33[ab]
11	10	13.50[ab]	5.00[ab]	3.33[ab]	4.00[ab]

[aa]*Not significant.*
[ab]*Significant.*

Table 3.
Observation results of dry red chilies storage by pressing treatment.

UNECE Standard 2012, which is 13.5%, but when referring to the SNI recommendation standard for chili 4480: 2016, then only up to the sixth week meets the standard.

3. Organoleptic parameters until the 10th week also showed a significant decrease different from the initial conditions. The scent level by week the tenth is at a score of 5.00, meaning it does not smell good anymore. The color parameter receives a score of 3.33, indicating that the hue becomes dull red rather than brownish, reducing the strength of attraction, while the taste receives a score of 4, indicating that it lacks spice.

4. The organoleptic test showed that up to the ninth week of quality, dry red cayenne pepper is still in acceptable condition (nothing exceeds a score of 3.33). Thus, using it as a raw material for the next stage of chili processing is still feasible.

5. Based on **Table 2** shows that changes in the conditions of the observation parameters compared to the initial conditions of the observations occurred in the fifth week for the moisture content parameter, the sixth week for the aroma parameter, the sixth week for the color parameter, and the fifth week for the taste parameter.

7. Roasting chili (*Capsicum annuum* L.) using Far-Infrared Radiation (IR)

Energy Infrared radiation is defined as electromagnetic waves with wavelengths ranging from 0.78 to 1000 m. It transfers heat more quickly than convection and conduction. When compared to standard hot air drying, IR radiation has lately gained a lot of attention due to its benefits in terms of Reduced drying time, increased energy transfer rate, energy savings, and higher product quality [22]. FIR heat applications are classified into four major groups according on their wavelength: baking, drying, thawing, and pasteurization are all methods of preserving food.

IR enters the exposed material after striking the surface of the substance. Because of radiation absorption, the vibration rises and concurrently generates heat at the material's surface and internal layers, increasing the heating rate [9]. The greatest depth of infrared penetration into agricultural systems output is 18 mm. As a result, the use of IR heating to achieve A high drying rate should concentrate on thin-layer drying—this treatment tried to investigate the feasibility of using FIR radiation to roast red chili. The findings concerning the red chili roasting procedure in this article are based on Fernando et al. [9] research.

8. Red chili samples

A 15 cm 5 cm electric Keramikemitter (660 W) was used to create FIR radiation (450–500°C surface temperature) on a single sheet of red chili pods (average length 10.54 cm, breadth 1.31 cm, and thickness 0.34 cm, bulk density 0.725 g/cm^3). With varied exposure times, at 3240, 3920, 5260, and 7188 W/m^2 FIR radiation intensities, the moisture content, temperature, and color change of chili pods were measured.

A prominent spice processing plant provided dried and factory-roasted red chili samples. The dried red chili samples were collected from the factory's unroasted bulk chili. For the studies, the samples were temporarily kept in polythene pouches (gauge 200) in the laboratory. The sample had a moisture content of 11% DB. The unroasted chili sample (250 g) was roasted for 25 min in a 24-kW drum roaster. To create a comparable hue using FIR radiation roasting, the roasted sample was utilized as a reference. Experiments with FIR radiation roasting was carried out using 12.191.16 g of unroasted red pepper sample.

9. Experimental setup

The FIR chili roasting setup's schematic design is illustrated in **Figure 6**.

A 15 cm 5 cm Keramik electric IR model with 660 W power was installed on top of the device to create FIR. The IR waves are focused onto the sample by an aluminum reflecting waveguide (30 cm height and 25.4 cm radius) that surrounds the FIR emitter and has a highly uniform IR dispersion across the cross-section. Chili (1919 1.16 g) was exposed to FIR radiation for 240 s by putting the sample at specified distances on a 5 mm thick hardwood sample tray (15 cm 5 cm). 7188, 5260, 3920, and the distance necessary to reach the appropriate FIR intensities. The results at 10 were 3240 W/m^2 measured at 15, 20, and 25 cm. These intensities were chosen because their relevance was highest at 1000 W/m^2 intervals.

The FIR heating unit was turned on for 5 min before placing the samples to ascertain the operational temperature. The intensity of FIR radiation was evaluated using an OPHIR FL205A Thermal Excimer Absorber Head (Ophir Optronics Inc., Wilmington, MA, USA), and the height adjustable stage was adjusted

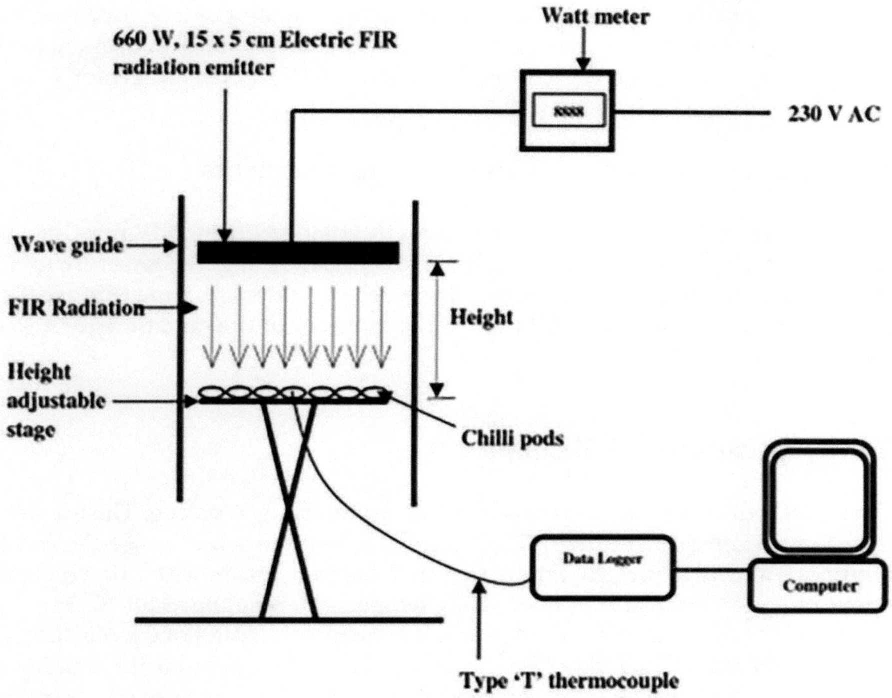

Figure 6.
The FIR red chili roasting apparatus is depicted schematically.

correspondingly. To eliminate FIR reflection during the experiment, chili pods were housed in a single layer on a wooden plate. Temperature and moisture content were measured during the FIR exposure. A single chili pod was used to measure color changes.

10. Moisture variation with FIR radiation

Chili had a starting moisture content of 11% db, and the weight loss of the roasting sample was monitored at predefined time intervals (0, 60, 120, 180 s) using an electronic scale (C.T.G. 602B-600, CITIZEN SCALE Inc. U.S.A.). On a height-adjustable platform, chili pods (12.191.16 g) were dispersed and subjected to FIR radiation.

11. Temperature and color variation of chili exposed to FIR radiation

T-type thermocouples implanted in three chili pods were used in each experiment to monitor and record the temperature of chili pods subjected to varying radiation intensities. Thermocouples were coupled to a data logger (TC-8, OMEGA, Japan), which was subsequently connected to a computer, as illustrated in **Figure 1**. Up to 240 s, the temperature was monitored in one-second increments. The color shift of chili pods roasted with FIR radiation was measured using a Chroma meter (Minolta CR 300, Japan). The results of three replicates were given as an average. The L*a*b* values of 20 chili pods were averaged after evaluating the color of a factory-roasted chili sample from Kundasale's finest spice processing plant. The figures served as the norm. The roasted chili color was contrasted with the FIR roasted chili color.

12. Moisture removal under different drying treatments

Figure 7 demonstrates the moisture content fluctuation during FIR roasting chili at various radiation intensities. In comparison to typical drying, the moisture loss of Chili with FIR heating demonstrated a linear relationship with time (**Figure 8**), showing logarithmic drying capabilities. As the intensity of the radiation grew, so did the rate of drying.

13. The temperature of chili samples

The temperature of chili is a crucial consideration during roasting. The use of the high-temperature short time (HTST) technique helps to achieve speedier roasting. **Figures 9** and **10** depict the fluctuation in chili temperature with FIR exposure at various radiation intensities. The roasting temperature was above 100°C. Even after 240 s of exposure at 3240 W/m^2, the FIR intensity chili did not exceed 100°C. According to the statistics, 7188 W/m^2 is the best FIR radiation intensity in industrial applications since it raises the temperature by 100°C in 60 s. Due to space constraints, it was difficult to achieve greater FIR radiation intensity. The FIR emitter's distance from the sample was measured. When employing FIR radiation at 7188 W/m^2, 10 cm would be the practically shortest distance permitting safe handling for chili roasting.

14. Color of chili with FIR radiation

The color of the chili pods was utilized to determine the roasting degree, and the difference in lightness (L*), redness (a*), and yellowness (b*) values was compared to a factory sample drum-roasted (**Figure 11**). L*a*b* values decreased after exposure to FIR radiation. **Figure 9** depicts chili's color change with a FIR radiation intensity of 7188 W/m^2. The factory roasted color values (L*a*b*) for chili are shown in **Figure 9** as

Time (t), s	3240 W/m2		3920 W/m2		5260 W/m2		7188 W/m2	
	MC	dMC/dt	MC	dMC/dt	MC	dMC/dt	MC	dMC/dt
0	11.00±0.00	0.00	11.00±0.00	0.00	11.00±0.00	0.00	11.00±0.00	0.00
60	10.08±0.01	0.02	8.59±0.02	0.04	8.78±0.01	0.04	9.02±0.02	0.03
120	8.69±0.02	0.02	6.66±0.01	0.03	5.67±0.02	0.05	6.24±0.01	0.05
180	6.84±0.01	0.03	4.73±0.01	0.03	3.45±0.01	0.04	2.68±0.02	0.06

MC (Moisture content %, dry basis), dMC/dt (Moisture removal rate)

Figure 7.
Moisture content and drying rate with varying sunlight intensity.

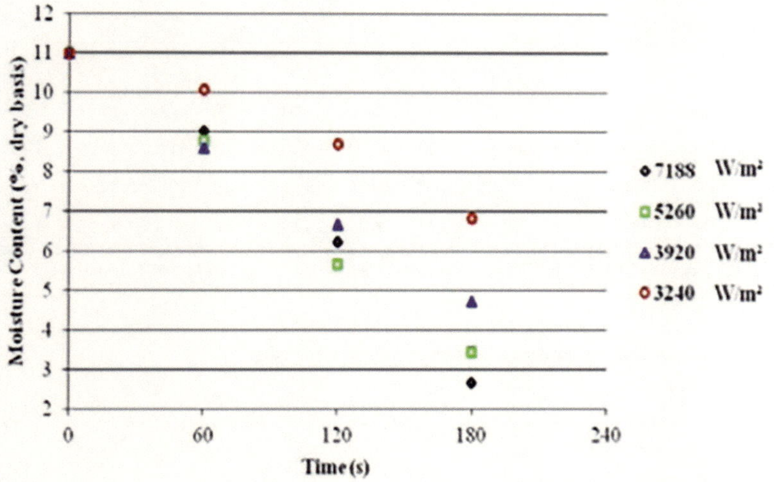

Figure 8.
The relationship between average chili moisture content and FIR heating time under various radiation intensities.

Time (s)	Temperature (°C)			
	3240 W/m² 25 cm*	3920 W/m² 20 cm*	5260 W/m² 15 cm*	7188 W/m² 10 cm*
0	24.80±0.00	24.80±0.00	24.80±0.00	24.80±0.00
60	68.85±8.28	80.77±7.98	86.55±4.31	100.03±4.6
120	80.56±5.94	88.27±4.67	96.51±0.24	108.82±7.46
180	88.48±4.53	96.25±3.42	100.81±2.79	120.97±7.79
240	92.87±3.85	101.47±5.18	108.01±3.75	132.25±7.62

*Distance between FIR emitter and the chilli sample

Figure 9.
Chili temperature varies with cooking time under different radiation intensity.

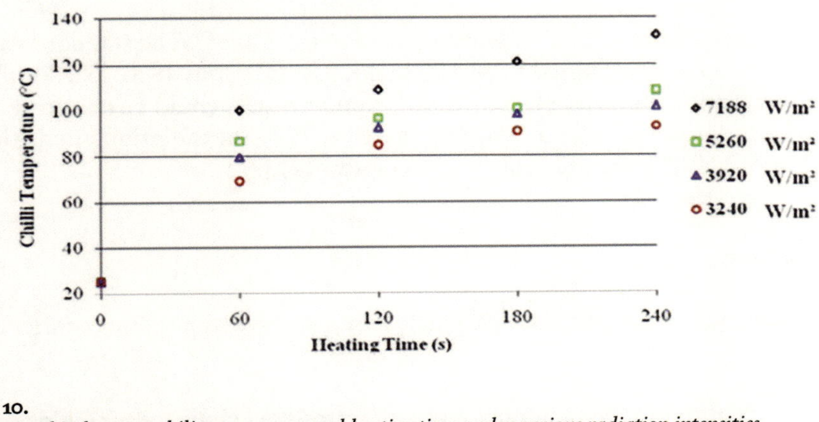

Figure 10.
The relationship between chili temperature and heating time under various radiation intensities.

Time (s)	3240 W/m²			3920 W/m²			5260 W/m²			7188 W/m²		
	L*	a*	b*	L*	a*	b*	L*	a*	b*	L*	a*	b*
0	34.83	14.19	64.80	34.83	14.19	64.80	34.83	14.19	64.80	34.83	14.19	64.80
60	33.56	14.80	60.74	32.63	13.12	56.41	32.03	10.88	52.86	30.93	5.59	46.07
120	30.85	9.64	47.50	31.82	10.16	52.09	30.39	4.63	43.53	29.58	1.27	39.62
180	29.17	3.89	38.90	29.41	4.52	40.25	29.51	1.48	39.37	29.39	1.03	38.97
240	27.80	1.28	33.65	28.72	1.32	36.78	29.88	1.10	40.55	29.58	1.48	39.59

Standard deviations for L*, a* and b* were in the range of 3.00-0.21, 6.75-0.09 and 15.34-0.60 respectively.
Standard (factory roasted) L*, a* and b* values were 30.73±1.76, 9.33±3.74 and 48.5±8.22 respectively.

Figure 11.
*L*a*b values vary with FIR exposure time at various radiation intensity.*

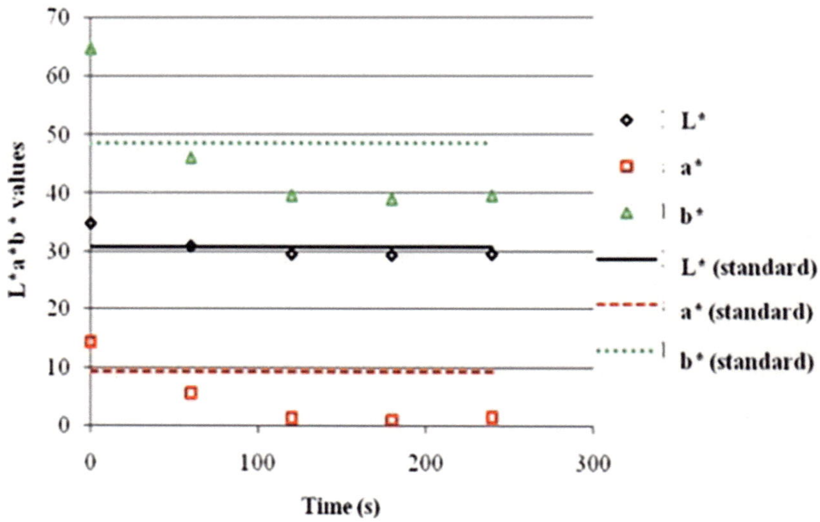

Figure 12.
*L*a*b values as a function of time and standard values of L*a*b at 7188 W/m² FIR the level of radiation.*

horizontal lines L* (standard), a* (standard), and b* (standard). The standard values for L*, a*, and b* were determined to be 30.73 (L*), 9.33 (a*), and 48.51 (b*). Similarly, with an FIR radiation intensity of 7188 W/m^2, similar results could be obtained in 60 s. Chili factory roasted color at 124, 117, as well as 107 s the radiation intensities measured were 3240, 3920, and 5260 W/m^2 (**Figure 12**) [22].

15. Conclusion

The conclusions obtained from this article based on several previous studies are as follows:

1. Price fluctuations in the consumer market for fresh red chilies occur owing to a variety of variables. First, because there is an abundance of fresh red chilies during harvest, the price of fresh red chilies falls to its lowest point. Second, because the

availability of fresh red chilies is limited, especially during the dry season, when demand for fresh red chilies increases, the price of fresh red chilies rises.

2. Overcoming the occurrence of high price fluctuations in fresh red chilies is accomplished by adjusting the time and location of planting fresh red chilies, improving the goods distribution system, implementing appropriate technology for fresh red chili products (drying, compressing, and roasting), and preparing a warehouse receipt system to store fresh red chili products resulting from post-harvest technology to meet demand for fresh red chilies, particularly during the dry season.

3. Drying and continuing to manufacture capable chili powder increases the shelf life of red cayenne pepper. Until the fifth week, the quality of cayenne pepper dry remains as before (excellent condition), whereas cayenne pepper just arrived 3–4 weeks with initial conditions.

4. Storage of red cayenne pepper in the form of dried chili is better compared to storage in the form of chili powder. For cayenne pepper, dry generally can last in good condition until the ninth week (still up to standard), whereas powdered red cayenne pepper survives until the sixth week.

5. The results showed that FIR radiation may successfully roast red chilies. In this study, the greatest FIR intensity employed was 7188 W/m^2. The proximity of the FIR emitter to the sample prevented further intensification of the sample.

6. The drum roaster needed 25 min to create roasted red chili, when the red chili was exposed to 7188 W/m^2, it retained the same color and moisture content. FIR radiation intensity for 60 s. The roasted color of red chili was attained at 124, 117, and 107 s at 3240, 3920, and 5260 W/m^2 radiation intensities, respectively the interpolated moisture levels were 8.38, 6.70, and 6.59% db, respectively.

7. As a result, FIR radiation might be employed to efficiently roast red sauce. Before adopting the method on an industrial scale, more research is needed to improve the quality of roasted red chili using FIR radiation.

Author details

Amos Lukas[1], Agustinus N. Kairupan[2*], Agung Hendriadi[1], Arief Arianto[1], Lamhot Parulian Manalu[1], Lanjar Sumarno[1], Joni Munarso[1], Mulyana Hadipernata[1], Huda M. Elmatsani[1], Bonnie O. Benyamin[1], Akhmad Junaidi[3], Mochammad Jusuf Djafar[1], Roosganda Elizabeth[3], Sahlan[1], Nasruddin[1], Puji Astuti[1], Subandrio[1], Heryoki Yohanes[1], Ermi E. Koeslulat[1], Eko Bhakti Susetyo[1], Suharto Ngudiwaluyo[4], Abdul Halik[5], Wahyu Purwanto[1], Guntur Haryanto[6], Sitti Ramlah[1], Noverina Sjafrina[1], Agus Budiyanto[1], Sari Intan Kailaku[1], Rienoviar[1], Alvi Yani[1], Nenie Yustiningsih[1], Himawan Adinegoro[1], Henky Henanto[1], Payung Layuk[1], Meivie Lintang[1], Gabriel H. Joseph[1], Derek Polakitan[2], Heri Wahyudianto[7], Joko Saptohadi[8], Kusumawati Dewi Budiarti[6], Taufik Hidayat[1], Josep Ginting[5], Amsal Rasyid[5] and August Polakitan[9]

1 Research Center for Agroindustry, National Research and Innovation Agency, Indonesia

2 Research Center for Animal Husbandry, National Research and Innovation Agency, Manado, Indonesia

3 Research Center for Cooperative, Corporation and Peoples' Economy, National Research and Innovation Agency, Indonesia

4 Directorate of Environment Maritime, Natural Resources, and Nuclear Policy, National Research and Innovation Agency, Indonesia

5 Research Center Domestic Government, National Research and Innovation Agency, Indonesia

6 Research Center for Process and Manufacturing Industry Technology, National Research and Innovation Agency, Indonesia

7 Regional Development Planning Agency Papua Agency, Indonesia

8 Regional Research and Innovation Agency for Kutai Kartanegara Regency, Indonesia

9 Research Center for Food Crops, National Research and Innovation Agency, Indonesia

*Address all correspondence to: audikairupan@gmail.com

References

[1] Wardhono A, Nasir MA, Qori'ah CG, Indrawati Y. Improving chili agribusiness policies to support food security: Evidence from Indonesian districts. In: IOP Conference Series: Earth and Environmental Science. 2021;**759**(1):1-8. DOI: 10.1088/1755-1315/759/1/012048

[2] Astuti FS, Wanto HS, Koesriwulandari K. Elasticity of demand for red pepper (*Capsicum annuum* L.) in the city of Surabaya. Jurnal Ilmiah Sosio Agribis. 2021;**21**(1):76-93. DOI: 10.30742/jisa21120211343

[3] Badan Pusat Statistik (BPS). Distribusi Perdagangan Komoditas Cabai Merah Indonesia. Jakarta: Badan Pusat Statistik; 2022

[4] Dudzinski J, Knap R. Price, volume and level of economic development as determinants of export value in countries and regions. Procedia Computer Science. 2022;**207**:3865-3874

[5] Rizaty MA. Indonesia's Cayenne Pepper Production Rose to 1.55 Million Tons in 2022. Indonesia Data. Id. Available from: https://dataindonesia.id/sektor-riil/detail/produksi-cabai-rawit-indonesia-naik-jadi-155-juta-ton-pada-2022; 2023

[6] Yusuf F, Rauf A, Halid A, Agribisnis J, Pertanian F. Cayenne pepper farming development strategy in Dungaliyo District, Gorontalo Regency. Agrinesia. 2018;**2**(2):133-144

[7] Bahar YH, Achdiyat, Promosiana A, Suharto YB, Ichniarscyah AN. Assess the Application of Post-Harvest Handling Technology of Red Cayenne Pepper (*Capsicum frutescens* L.). Bogor: Politeknik Pembangunan Pertanian; 2022

[8] Bahar YH. Analysis of drying efficiency process and producing dried and powder chilli for improving the durability. Jurnal Agroekoteknologi Dan Agribisnis. 2017;**1**(1):39-47

[9] Fernando AJ, Amaratunga KSP, Priyadarshana LBMDL, Galahitiyawa DDK, Karunasinghe KGWU. Using far-infrared radiation to roast chilli (*Capsicum annum* L.). Agricultural Research in the Tropics. 2014;**25**(2):180-187

[10] Bakar A, Tjahjohutomo R. Post-Harvest Technological Innovation of BioIndustrial Agriculture. Center for Research and Development of Post-harvest Agriculture; 2015

[11] Asgar A, Musaddad D, Setyabudi DA, Hassan ZH. Ozonization technology to maintain the freshness of chili cultivar kencana during storage. Jurnal Penelitian Pascapanen Pertanian|. 2015;**12**(1):21-27

[12] Jamilah M, Fadilah R. Uji Kualitas Bubuk Cabai Rawit (*Capsicum frutescens*) Berdasarkan Berat Tumpukan dan lama Pengeringan Menggunakan cabinet dryer test quality of Cayenne pepper (*Capsicum frutescens*) powder based on stack weight and long drying using cabinet dryer. Jurnal Pendidikan Teknologi Pertanian. 2019;**5**:98-107

[13] Ajuebor F, Aworanti OA, Agbede OO, Agarry SE, Afolabi TJ, Ogunleye OO. Optimization of the drying process and modeling of the drying kinetics and quality attributes of dried chili pepper (*Capsicum frutescens* L.). Trends in Sciences. 2022;**19**(17):1-21. DOI: 10.48048/tis.2022.5752

[14] Jangde PK, Singh A, Arjunan TV. A overview of efficient solar drying processes. Environmental Science and Pollution Research.

2022;**29**(34):50970-50983. DOI: 10.1007/s11356-021-15792-4.202

[15] Maryana YE, Saputra D, Priyanto G, Yuliati K. A review of the inflated solar dryer for improving the quality of agricultural products. IOP Conference Series: Earth and Environmental Science. 2023;**1160**(1):1-10. DOI: 10.1088/1755-1315/1160/1/012075

[16] Meghwar BL, Khan A, Lakhiar IA, Mirani AA, Daper MS, Kalroo MW. Drying red chilies in a solar tunnel, a solar-cum gas dryer, and in the open sun. Pakistan Journal of Agricultural Research. 2023;**36**(1):63-70. DOI: 10.17582/JOURNAL.PJAR/2022/36.1.63.70

[17] Vishwakarma A, Sinha S, Malik P. A solar dryer study to reduce postharvest losses. In: Lecture Notes in Mechanical Engineering. Singapore: Springer Nature; 2022. DOI: 10.1007/978-981-16-8341-1_28

[18] Getahun E, Gabbiye N, Delele MA, Fanta SW, Vanierschot M. Chili drying in a two-stage solar tunnel: Drying characteristics, performance, product quality, and carbon footprint analysis. Solar Energy. 2021;**230**:73-90. DOI: 10.1016/J.SOLENER.2021.10.016

[19] Alves-Filho O, Eikevik T, Mulet A, Garau C, Rossello C. The kinetics of mass transfer of red pepper under air freeze drying. Drying Technology. 2007;**25**(7-8):1155-1161. DOI: 10.1080/07373930701438469

[20] Gutiérrez BLC, Cardozo CJM, Rojano BA. Effect of the freeze-drying on the functional properties of Rocoto chili pepper. Artículo Científico. 2017;**20**(1):111-119

[21] Setyabudi DA, Broto W, Jamal IB. The effect of immersion in benomyl solution on the freshness of chili pepper (*Capsicum annum* L. Var. Kencana) at low temperature storage and space. Jurnal Penelitian Pascapanen Pertanian. 2016;**13**(2):53-62

[22] Saengrayap R, Tansakul A, Mittal GS. Effect of far-infrared radiation assisted microwave-vacuum drying on drying characteristics and quality of red chili. Journal of Food Science and Technology. 2015;**52**(5):2610-2621. DOI: 10.1007/s13197-014-1352-4

Chapter 3

Olive Oil: Challenges in a Changing Environment

Bukola Margaret Popoola, Olusolabomi Jose Adefioye and Comfort Tosin Olateru

Abstract

Olive oil is a liquid fat from a traditional tree crop of the Mediterranean region, obtained by pressing whole olives (the fruit of *Olea europaea*; family Oleaceae) and then extracting the oil. It has a variety of usage such as cosmetics, cooking, medicine, fuel for traditional lamps and soaps. Olive oil is highly beneficial to life, and it is proven to contain large amounts of antioxidants which are biologically active and of great health benefit. However, due to unmitigated climate change, resulting from rising greenhouse gas emission worldwide and especially in Europe, olive oil production is being challenged. There is a prediction of a 30% drop in olive oil production in the southern region of Spain (Spain is the current highest olive oil producer) by 2100, this would mutilate the production of olive oil and the olive sector. Subject to the continuous rise in temperature, as a result of the deadly heat wave that has been plaguing most of Europe, the majority of the non-irrigated olive tree plantations may become unsuitable to cultivate olives. There is therefore an urgent need to mitigate this negative impact on this highly beneficial Mediterranean diet by employing suitable modeled adaptation.

Keywords: antioxidants, olive oil, greenhouse gas, temperature, inflammation, irrigation

1. Introduction

The traditional tree crop found in the Mediterranean Basin, olives (fruit of *Olea europaea*; family Oleaceae), is the source of olive oil, produced basically by pressing the whole olives and extracting the oil, such fruit is as shown in **Figure 1** [1]. Olive trees were known to be cultivated in Crete, by the Late Minoan (1500 BC), and possibly as early as the Early Minoan [2]. It is worth noting that olive trees cultivation in Crete became explicitly intense during the post-palatial period, subsequently playing a salient role in the island's economy, just as it was across the Mediterranean [3]. From the eight millennium BC thenceforward, olive trees have been grown around the Mediterranean basin, in Asia Minor and near Syria. Today, olive oil is extremely abundant in Asia Minor, however, it seems to have spread from Syria to Türkiye, subsequently to Greece and Crete. Eventually with the establishment of Greek colonies in other parts of the Mediterranean, farming of olive was brought to places like

Figure 1.
Olives fruits. Source: [1].

Spain from where it has continued to spread all over the Roman Empire [4], however, today, it is popular around the world.

It is of great interest to know that olive oil is highly rich in fatty acids and functional bioactive compounds like Phospholipids, Carotenoids, Phenolics, and Tocopherols with various biological activities, these contents are responsible for possible potential health benefits of olive oil [5]. They also contribute to the taste and distinct flavor of olive oil. Furthermore, they are known for the remedy of some tropical disorders such as malaria and fever [6]. Olives are seldom utilized in their natural form because of their bitterness, nonetheless, they are ingested either as table olives or oil [5].

Authors have claimed that oleuropein a phytoconstituent in olive, have antibacterial properties, some also assert that oleuropein could act against toxins produced by *Staphylococcus aureus* and possibly have antiviral effect against hepatitis viruses and herpes. Moreover, there is the proposition of the potential antiviral activity of olive leaf extract against the virus that causes acquired immunodeficiency syndrome [7].

Studies have also shown that polyphenols might inhibit the development and reproduction of *Klebsiella pneumonia*, *Bacillus cereus*, *Escherichia coli*, and *Salmonella typhi*. Hence, olive oil has been reported to have potential antibacterial properties for respiratory and intestinal infections [8].

However, in spite of the great environment for cultivation of olive oil, one of the greatest challenges of our time is climate change. Impacts from a changing climate will certainly affect the natural world as well as the built environment, thereby giving rise to a new comprehensive approach to adaptation. All resolve towards assessments of environmental impacts, future planning of our cities, built environment, setting standards and codes, identifying risks, are usually carried out based on data and knowledge of the past. However, the future tends to be obviously different, with a changing environment due to challenges faced, from a degrading ecosystem to a severe change in the climate, this will literally force a reconsideration of the knowledge system. In the face of a rapid changing climate, the ability of a system to absorb surprises and disturbances, and for the moment accomplishing a condition of dynamic equilibrium that will permit systems evolve and grow while keeping their coherence is entirely complex global issues.

DOI: http://dx.doi.org/10.5772/intechopen.113004

Nutrient	Amount
Total fat	93.7 g
Fatty acids	15.4 g
Stigmasterol	1.02 mg
Campesterol	5.68 mg
Beta-sitosterol	126 mg
Beta-sitostanol	2.55 mg
Delta-5-avenasterol	23.1 mg
Source: [8]	

Table 1.
The nutritional content of 100 g of olive oil.

2. Types of olive oil

Olive oil is of various types: virgin olive oil (edible), extra virgin olive oil (edible), refined olive oil (edible), olive-pomace oils (non-edible) and lampante olive oil (non-edible) [8]. **Table 1** highlights the nutritional value of olive oil.

3. Potential properties and benefits of olive oil: uses of olive oil and health benefit

Studies have shown that a phytoconstituent in olive called Oleuropein has antibacterial properties against bacteria, including mycoplasma. Moreover, there is the possibility of the phenolic chemicals in olive oil to break down bacterial membranes, hence showing antibacterial activities. Several researchers also state that oleuropein may act against toxins produced by *Staphylococcus aureus* and could have an antiviral effect against herpes and hepatitis viruses. Likewise, the potential antiviral activity of olive leaf extract against the virus that causes acquired immunodeficiency syndrome has been proposed [7].

Olive oil has been shown to have potential antibacterial properties for respiratory and intestinal infections [8]. Nevertheless, this needs further confirmation.

Researchers have also found that consuming extra virgin olive oil might reduce liver tissue damage in animal models. Furthermore, the combined therapy of olive oil and camel milk in animal models demonstrated possible liver protective effects in drug-induced liver toxicity due to their potent antioxidant action [8]. However, it is worth noting that diseases such as liver disease can be very challenging and need real diagnosis and treatment by experts.

Some scientists researched on the impact of olive oil on colon cancer. From their investigations they suggested that the presence of antioxidants, fatty acids and phenolic compounds in olive oil might play an important role in reducing the risk of colon cancer [7].

Essentially, there are various properties of olive oil including being a potential antioxidant, having potential anti-inflammatory, anti-microbial, anti-atherogenic, anti-tumor, anti-platelet aggregation activities. Olive oil might help in lowering blood pressure, they might act as an as well as liver-protective immunity enhancer, wound healing, anti-allergic agent. They might also have brain-protective activity.

4. Climate change

The word Climate, indicates the long-term regional or global average of rainfall, humidity, and temperature patterns over seasons, years or decades. Generally, weather could change in just a few hours, on the other hand climate changes over longer timeframes. Climate change is the notable variation of average weather conditions being, for example, drier, wetter, or warmer—over some decades or longer. However, *it is the longer-term trend that distinguishes natural weather variability from climate change.*

It is worth noting that human activities could lead to atmospheric composition change either directly (through emissions of particles or gases) or indirectly (through atmospheric chemistry). Anthropogenic emissions are drivers of changes in well-mixed greenhouse gases (WMGHG; mainly carbon dioxide, methane, nitrous oxide, and the chlorofluorocarbons) concentrations during the industrial era.

The earth's climate is changing and the global climate is projected to continue to change over this century and beyond. The extent of climate change surpassing the next few decades will primarily depend on the amount of greenhouse (heat-trapping) gases emitted globally and on the remaining uncertainty in the sensitivity of the Earth's climate to those emissions [9]. Hence, global annual averaged temperature rise could be limited to 2°C or less, especially with significant reductions in the emissions of greenhouse gases (GHGs). Interestingly, without major depletions in these emissions, the rise in annual average global temperatures, relative to preindustrial times, can possibly reach 5°C or more by the end of this century [9].

Furthermore, there is the continuous rapid changing of the global climate in comparison to the pace of the natural variations in climate that have occurred throughout earth's history. It has been observed that trends in- sea level rise, globally averaged temperature, upper-ocean heat content, arctic sea ice, depth of seasonal permafrost thaw, land-based ice melt, and other climate variables give consistent evidence of a warming planet [9]. These observations are strong, solid and established by multiple, independent research groups around the world. The **Figure 2** below is a

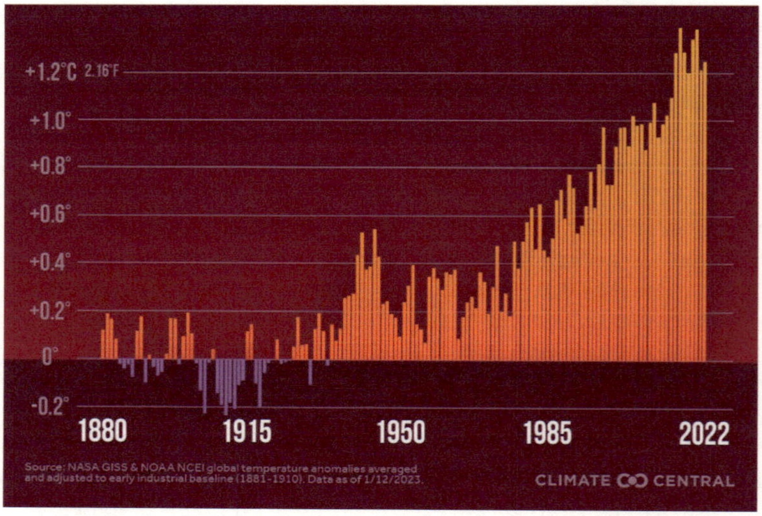

Figure 2.
Global average temperature anomalies, departure from 1881 to 1910. Source: [9].

representation of global average temperature anomalies; it shows that from the 1880s global average temperature has warmed approximately 1°C.

The plot in **Figure 2** reveals how much global annual average temperatures for the years 1880–2022 have been above or below the 1881–1910 average. Temperatures for years warmer than the early industrial baseline are shown in red; temperatures for years cooler than the baseline are shown in purple.

Many think climate change basically means a condition or situation of warmer temperatures, however, temperature rise is only the beginning of the story. Since the earth is a system, where everything is connected, changes in one area could influence changes in all other areas. Therefore, the following consequences among others on climate change has been revealed; water scarcity, intense droughts, rising sea levels, severe fires, melting polar ice, catastrophic storms, flooding and declining biodiversity.

Above all, climate change can also affect human health as discussed earlier, it can affect housing, safety, work and even ability to grow food. Conditions such as saltwater intrusion and sea-level rise have advanced greatly to the point where we have whole communities relocate, also there is also the risk of famine as a result of protracted droughts.

4.1 Roles of olive trees on climate

In Spain, this current crop occupies 14% of the country's agricultural area, representing nearly half (45%) of world production (Alonso, 2022). As obtainable with any large plantation of trees, large olive groves areas, absorb a considerable amount of CO_2 [10]. It was estimated that "each olive tree, on average, absorbs 30 kg of CO_2 per year (considering the fact that there are larger and smaller olive trees) this makes the olive grove an important factor in curbing climate change".

Olive trees can to certain extent mitigate the effects of climate change via their absorption of CO_2, however they are often victims of climate change [10]. It is worth noting that increasing GHG emissions are causing rise in temperatures and in the frequency of dire weather events such as storms, droughts or unseasonal temperatures [11]. Findings from a recent research showed that climate change is expected to cut down on the area where olive growing is possible in Andalusia, being Spain's largest oil-producing region, as well as other possible olive-growing regions primarily due to hotter and drier weather in autumn and summer [12]. The absence of rain and anticipated dry spells will definitely bring about water stress to the olive tree and, at the same time temperature increase will result in heat stress. This 'stress' destroys trees physiologically, compromising flowering and thus olive production [10].

Olive trees have been judged as durable mythologically and historically [1]. Nonetheless, irregular seasonal changes as well as temperature increases are affecting crucial processes that result in a good season. Olive flowering is the most phenological process affected by climate in the olive orchard, this usually occurs in the season of spring, its onset is extremely susceptible to temperature as well as to the period where olive fruit mature and ripens, during mid to late summer. It's been observed in recent years, the advancement of flowering and the acceleration of ripening, this usually causes the flowers to drop before they are set into fruits. Moreover, there has been a decline in the number of olives per tree as well as change in the quality of these olives oil. Furthermore, the risk of phenological stress due lack of water resources and high temperatures in summer is on the increase. All the above mentioned factors gear towards less productive harvests [1, 13].

Some researchers at the Consejo Superior de Investigaciones Científicas (CSIC), built a biophysical model called OliveCan 2.0 by virtue of the challenge of making dependable forecasts on the response of olive groves to climate change, this model simulates a number of the processes that may occur as a result of the effects of climate change. The model reveals, for instance, the reduction in flowering percentage in a scenario of elevated temperatures or the propensity of flowering dates to proceed in weeks or months in this same scenario with higher temperatures [1].

Another group of researchers who happen to come from the University of Cordoba in Spain and the Research Center for Geo-Space Science (CICGE) in Portugal, predicted likely changes in the contemporary distribution of diverse olive tree varieties. Two varieties, presently constitute 80% of the whole Andalusian olive crops: hojiblanca (20%) and picual (60%), being the most versatile and productive. Nevertheless, for centuries olive producers have chosen some other varieties more adapted to difficult terrain, soil types, or to certain local climates [14].

Furthermore, it's been discovered that these local varieties are at more risk of disappearing. According to Arenas-Castro, those local varieties have specified needs that are spatially restricted since the varieties are themselves more restricted an example he cites is nevadillo, a variety presently cultivated in Sierra Morena, near Cordoba. The precise climatic conditions to cultivate it would have completely vanished by 2100 [14].

However, other experts are not exactly sure of the fate of these trees under climate change, for instance, Diego Barranco, an olive cultivation and olive genetics expert at the University of Cordoba, expressed that olive trees are unlikely to die off just like that because they are extremely hardy. He reiterated that such dire climate changes are not anticipated in the medium term.

Nonetheless, growers most likely will substitute struggling varieties with more adaptable ones. Barranco predicts that these changes are bound to be slow-paced, thereby making it unlikely that any variety is completely lost [14].

4.2 Effect of climate change on olive tree

Spain has been said to be the largest producer and exporter of olive oil in the world, even ahead of Greece and Italy [15]. Climate change has adversely affected the world over the years. Of the most recent impact is that on the production of olive oil in Europe. It is worth noting that olive groves have actually emerged with the Mediterranean climate and are famous for their resistance to water scarcity. There has been an incessant plaguing by this deadly heat wave which has resulted to a direct reduction in olive oil production in most of Europe such as in Italy and Spain.

Besides, recent years have evidenced that even the olive tree, a symbolically resilient tree, may perhaps be one of the crops grievously affected by the effects of climate change, endangering a millennia-old source of culture, subsistence and commerce [13].

Such as been observed with olive trees submerged in floodwater (**Figure 3**). Extreme weather events and shifting climate patterns have caused tremendous heavy rainfall in olive-producing regions. As olive trees are adapted for dry soil conditions, this can cause crop failure and root-rot.

Figure 3.
Olive trees submerged in floodwater. Source: [1].

4.3 Effects of climate change on olive oil industry

Some researchers from the CICGE in Portugal and the University of Cordoba in Spain tried to investigate how well the olive industry will adapt to the effects of climate change. They discovered that warmer winters and increased drought will reduce the number of land available to cultivate commercially relevant olive varieties, reducing production by 30% before the end of the century [16].

It is worth noting that the climate of Andalusian favors olive trees cultivation. They are resistant to drought and heat, these are common during summers. The winters, however, are cold, though temperatures rarely drop below −8°C, the tree's lower tolerance limit. In the case of flowering olive trees also need a bit of a chill during winter in order to flower during spring, a physiological necessity known as vernalization.

In order to evaluate the response of current olive plantations to climate change, the species distribution modeling (SDM), an algorithm-based computer method was used by the researchers. This tool is often used to forecast what areas are adequate for the presence of a particular species based on environmental features. Hence, they could predict the future evolution of the most common olive varieties by combining high-resolution climate projections with SDM and extremely detailed satellite imagery.

However, [16], reported that "being the first time this method was developed, the model was detailed and tailored to specified olive varieties that were cultivated commercially". They could correlate each tree's specific location with its predicted levels of temperature, precipitation, evaporation, and so on.

The researchers discovered that the most salient factor that will reduce olive production is reduction in rainfall and loss of soil humidity. It was predicted that five of eight Andalusian provinces were to lose olive production, with decreases in fit land for olive production of 25% in Cadiz, 29% in Seville, and a lesser proportion in other regions. They also realized that some mountain areas will become better suited for cultivating olive trees, as these normally colder regions will become more temperate. Nevertheless, these areas are, for the most part, natural reserves or presently occupied by other crops.

5. Possible adaptations

A period of agricultural and, therefore, social change and uncertainty could lie ahead. There is the need to work, adapt and protect landscapes that are as dear as they are tied to our Mediterranean past and present.

Adaptations exist for both short and long term scenarios, for the short term scenario, there is an increased possibility of crop failure, while looking at the long term effect, the risk is expressed in an overall reduction in yield quality and quantity [10]. Going by the OliveCan 2.0 projection wherein flowering take place earlier in the year when the weather is warmer, growers can adapt in the short term by altering their patterns of cropping. Large investments is required in irrigation as well as in the adjustment of the times of the year of its application in order to prevent water stress [17]. However, there could be situations that might not be so easy to adapt to. For instance there was a small localized tornado in Mallorca in the year 2020, which wiped about 80% of the oil crop on the island of the largest producer of this oil crop.

Extreme weather events like these—more frequent cold or heat waves, new suboptimal average growing temperatures, and acute and unforeseen pest outbreaks will require utmost transitions in olive farming. In order to get by with these changes, it will be expedient to investigate the most robust and resilient olive varieties, conserve soil health to maintain or improve water retention, consider intercropping techniques, in which different species are grown at the same time on the same area of land, and, in some instances, even shift the area of olive orchards to more conducive areas altogether [1]. As a result of the latter, it could be argued that, as areas in California, New Zealand or central Europe can conveniently accommodate olive groves, the competitiveness of the Mediterranean coastal strips will decline, and with it Spain's leading status in global olive oil production [1].

6. Conclusion

Olive oil production is currently being challenged due to unmitigated climate change, resulting from rising GHG emission worldwide and especially in Europe. Although, researchers have observed that as obtainable with any large plantation of trees, large olive groves areas, absorb a considerable amount of CO_2, with the emphasis that, it has been estimated that "each olive tree, on average, absorbs 30 kg of CO_2 per year (considering the fact that there are larger and smaller olive trees) this makes the olive grove an important factor in curbing climate change". Despite this postulation, the overall effect of climate change on olive tree and olive industry is still overwhelming despite adaptive measures.

Hence the urgent need to mitigate this negative impact on this highly beneficial Mediterranean diet is needful via the employment of suitable modeled adaptation such as changing cropping patterns, irrigation etc. It will also be expedient to investigate the most robust and resilient olive varieties, conserve soil health to maintain or improve water retention, consider intercropping techniques, in which different species are grown at the same time on the same area of land, and, in some instances, even shift the area of olive orchards to more conducive areas altogether. These measures may therefore anticipate the effects of climate change on olive crops and provide early estimates of fruit production, at local and regional scales, as well as forming the basis of adaptation strategies.

Acknowledgements

I would like to acknowledge the staff and students of the department of Biological Sciences, Ajayi Crowther University, Oyo, Oyo State, Nigeria.

Conflict of interest

The authors declare no conflict of interest.

Author details

Bukola Margaret Popoola[1*], Olusolabomi Jose Adefioye[2] and Comfort Tosin Olateru[3]

1 Department of Biological Sciences, Ajayi Crowther University, Oyo, Oyo State, Nigeria

2 Department of Biological Sciences, Kings University, Ode-omu, Osun State, Nigeria

3 Department of Microbiology, Polytechnic of Ibadan, Ibadan, Oyo State, Nigeria

*Address all correspondence to: bm.popoola@acu.edu.ng

References

[1] Alonso IO. 2022. How will a Changing Climate Affect Olive Oil Trees? Food unfolded EIT Food. Available from: https://www.foodunfolded.com/article/how-will-a-changing-climate-affect-olive-trees#

[2] Riley FR. Olive oil production on bronze age Crete: nutritional properties, processing methods, and storage life of Minoan olive oil. Oxford Journal of Archaeology. 2002;**21**(1):63-75

[3] Moody J, Rackham O, Rapp G. Environmental archaeology of prehistoric NW crete. Journal of Field Archaeology. 1996;**23**(3):273-297. DOI: 10.2307/530483

[4] Kapellakis IE. Olive oil history, production and by-product management. Reviews in Environmental Science and Bio/Technology. 2008;7(1):1-26. DOI: 10.1007/s11157-007-9120-9. S2CID 84992505

[5] Ghanbari R, Anwar F, Alkharfy KM, Gilani AH, Saari N. Valuable nutrients and functional bioactives in different parts of olive (*Olea europaea* L.) - a review. International Journal of Molecular Sciences. 2012;**13**(3):3291-3340. Available from: https://pubmed.ncbi.nlm.nih.gov/22489153/

[6] Singh R. 2022. Olive Oil: Uses, Benefits, Side Effects and More! Available from: https://pharmeasy.In/blog/author/rajeevisingh645/

[7] Yousefi Z, Rezaeigolestani M, Hashemi M. Biological properties of olive oil. Journal of Human Environment and Health Promotion. 2018;**4**(2):50-54. Available from: https://oaji.net/articles/2019/4672-1562994176.pdf

[8] Bilal RM, Liu C, Zhao H, Wang Y, Farag MR, Alagawany M, et al. Olive oil: Nutritional applications, beneficial health aspects and its prospective application in poultry production. Frontiers Pharmacology. 2021;**12**:723040. DOI: 10.3389/fphar.2021.723040

[9] Climate Change Knowledge Portal for Development Practitioners and Policy Makers. Available from: https://climateknowledgeportal.worldbank.org/overview

[10] Asociación Española de Municipios del Olivo. Impacto del Cultivo del Olivo sobre el CC. Efecto del CC sobre la estabilidad del mercado del aceite de oliva en España. Consultado el 11 de Abril 2021. 2019

[11] Instituto Internacional de Investigación sobre Políticas Alimentarias. Cambio Climático: El impacto en la agricultura y los costos de adaptación. Consultado el 8 de Abril 2021. 2009

[12] Science of the Total Environment. Projected climate changes are expected to decrease the suitability and production of olive varieties in southern Spain. Consultado el 8 de Abril 2021. 2020

[13] Eos. Climate Change Will Reduce Spanish Olive Oil Production. Consultado el 10 de Abril 2021. 2020

[14] Barbuzano J. Climate change will reduce Spanish olive oil production. EOS 101. 2020. DOI: 10.1029/2020EO141586. Published on 19 March 2020

[15] European Commission. Producing 69% of the world's production, the EU is the largest producer of olive oil. Consultado el 10 de Abril 2021. 2020

[16] Arenas-Castro S, Gonçalves JF, Moreno M, Villar R. Projected climate

changes are expected to decrease the suitability and production of olive varieties in southern Spain. Science of the Total Environment. 2020;**709**:136161. ISSN 0048-9697. DOI: 10.1016/j.scitotenv.2019.136161

[17] Sputnik. El cambio climático amenaza al olivo y al aceite tal como los conocemos hasta ahora. Consultado el 10 de Abril 2021. 2020

Section 3

Researches and Recent Advances

Chapter 4

The Role of Extension and Education in Agricultural Development: Empirical Evidence from Iran

Neda Seyedan, Iraj Malek Mohammadi, Jamal Farajollah Hoseini and Reza Moghaddasi

Abstract

For several years, economic sanctions imposed by the US have created considerable pressure on Iran's economy. Thus, Iran has continuously been seeking ways that improve productivity progress in order to acquire greater production by consuming fewer resources. This study aimed to explain the design of agricultural extension in the resistive economics development in Iran and present a practical model. The general approach of the present research is quantitative and inferential and has a mixed nature. Indeed, this investigation is semi-experimental in terms of the possibility of controlling variables, and data collection has been performed through the assessment of documents, context, and library. For sampling, the stratified random sampling method was used, while the sample size (151) was determined using the modified Cochran's formula. Structural equation modeling (SEM) and LISREL software were applied to analyze the collected data, and finally, the structural equation modeling was achieved through regression and path analyzes. The validity of the questionnaire through expert opinion and average variance extracted (AVE) index, and the reliability of the questionnaire through Cronbach's alpha coefficient (89%) were obtained. The findings of the goodness-of-fit test for the deterrent factor of agricultural extension affecting resistive economics show that the set of independent variables could explain 61–83% of the probability of variance of the dependent variable. For the leading factor of agricultural extension affecting the resistive economics, between 68.8 and 99.6%, and for the factor of resistive economics affecting the agricultural development sector, between 69.1 and 99.8% were calculated.

Keywords: resistive economics, extension, education, agricultural, development

1. Introduction

A disrupted economy causes many problems for society. Nowadays, increasing population growth has increased the need for agricultural products and, subsequently, basic resources used for production. Also, economic sanctions have been known as a disruptive factor to economic growth in general and agricultural development in particular. In contrast, resistive economics is the concept and strategy that has been considered in the case of international sanctions. Resistive economics deals with the methods of economic development in the form of enlarging dimensions of the economy. In order to improve economic variables, and extend economic capacities, improved economics is the opportunities and evolution in the context of economics. It is recommended that the capacity of investment be concentrated in the field of agriculture, and the presence of farmers in the economy is needed. In this regard, the existence of economic planning plays an important role in the regulation of supply, demand, optimum utilization of available resources, and production factors [1].

On this basis, it can be concluded that agricultural economics is associated with the methods of optimal use of natural resources in agriculture [2]. Agriculture, if there is an advance in the next stage there, becomes a driving force of community development [3]. Extenstion trends and policies in the world indicate that at the current stage, a series of forces and factors that themselves are signs of vast forces in society affect the evolution and extension in terms of conception, politics, and structure [4]. The need for agricultural extension stems from the belief that the life of villagers and farmers should be improved. The deep gap that exists between the current and desired situations is mainly filled by the use of science and technology in economic and social activities and through changes in the behavior of the villagers. In this regard, agricultural extension plays a vital role. Nowadays, one of the most important needs agriculture sector is the increased economic power [5].

One of the necessary measures to design a model of progress is to have a strategic plan for the development and progress of the country. It is necessary to be aware of the current situation according to internal factors (strengths and weaknesses) and external factors (opportunities and threats); the correct strategic analysis should be done [6].

2. Theoretical framework

In world economic literature, resistive economics is a new concept, although it is less emphasized [7]. Resistive economics means the pressure of other countries and the attempt to control and mitigate these pressures in ideal conditions and turn threats into opportunities. Also, it can reduce dependencies and emphasize the benefits of domestic production and self-reliance efforts [8]. Resistive Economics is an approach to counteract economic and strategic sanctions, especially in cases where the exports and imports of a country are limited [9]. Increasing the need for crops due to some factors, such as urban development, income growth, changing food consumption patterns, the need to increase the productivity of agricultural lands, and also the resources available to farmers, is vital. Meanwhile, the existence of economic planning has an important role in regulating the supply, demand, and optimal use of available resources and factors of production [1].

"Terms and theories can be mentioned that are close and similar to it. The theory of economic resilience is one of them. State that the term economic is used in two senses: First, the ability of the economy to recover quickly from destructive external economic shocks and, Second, the ability of economics to withstand the effects of these shocks [10]." Resistance economics also has positive aspects, such as the progress of science, and more productions, and also has many aspects such as reducing. "In Iran, agricultural development is still a fundamental means of poverty alleviation,

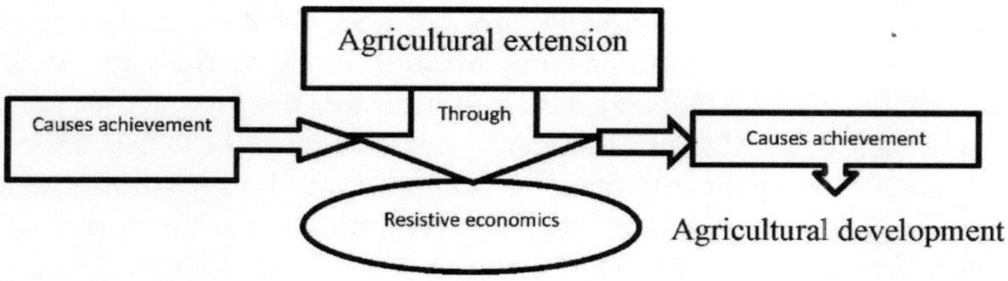

Figure 1.
Role of agricultural extension affecting in agricultural development.

economic development and, in general, sustainable development [11]. The agricultural sector in Iran has played a key role in providing food security by relying on domestic resources, providing foreign exchange through increased exports, supplying the raw materials needed by the industry, and helping to develop dependent productive activities, efficient employment [12]. In resistive economics, the opportunities, capabilities, strengths and potentials of the agricultural sector should be used and the threats that have driven farmers out of the field should be turned into opportunities [13]". From the point of view of economists, resistive economics is a space to face dependent independence and consumerism. Such an economy is not passive and stands against the goals of economic domination and he tries to change his economic structure based on his own goals and ideology data and tries to put the economy in line with its values and attitudes [14].

In **Figure 1** shows that the expansion of agriculture extension through resistive economics as a solution to the problems of the agricultural sector leads to agricultural development.

"In Iran, agricultural development is still a fundamental means of poverty alleviation, economic development and, in general, sustainable development [11]. The agricultural sector in Iran has played a key role in providing food security by relying on domestic resources, providing foreign exchange through increased exports, supplying the raw materials needed by the industry, and helping to develop dependent productive activities, efficient employment [12]. In resistive economics, the opportunities, capabilities, strengths and potentials of the agricultural sector should be used and the threats that have driven farmers out of the field should be turned into opportunities [13]." From the point of view of economists, resistive economics is a space to face dependent independence and consumerism. Such an economy is not passive and stands against the goals of economic domination and he tries to change his economic structure based on his own goals and ideology data and tries to put the economy in line with its values and attitudes [14].

"With the assistance of resistive economics, which aims to empower farmers, water, land, and available facilities can be used to the greatest extent and can be used to turn threats into opportunities and strengths (SWOT). So, resistive economics with the extension of agriculture has common goals about farming and empowering farmers, and creating a balance between deterrent and leading factors [15]. The opportunities, capabilities, strengths, and potential of the agricultural sector should be used, and the threats that have pushed farmers out of the field into turned into an opportunity; strengths must be strengthened and weaknesses reduced to reduce pressure, and strengthen the contribute leading factors [16]."

"Necessity and importance of paying attention to the resistive economy in the field of agriculture means expanding efforts to make maximum use of existing facilities to produce strategic and basic products to reduce dependence on foreign countries, increase productivity as much as possible, produce goods that reduce foreign dependence provide the necessary input in a complete and timely manner and identify problems and challenges [17]." Such a situation indicates the pivotal role of resistive economics in the agricultural sector in recent years and reveals the existence of a targeted plan for the extension and resistive economics in the agricultural sector [18]. For data analysis, they have used statistical and structural equation modeling (SEM) [19]. Also, they showed the relationship between variables and a conceptual model (Raza et al. 2019). The main purpose of SEM is significant for modeling the extension of agriculture to achieve sustainable development. The hypotheses of the research were assessed by studying relationship between variables and direct and indirect effects, and then they were analyzed by SEM analysis. After data extracting, statistics and structural equivalence using SPSSV19, R, and AMOSv23 softwares were described.

3. Methods

"The present work is a mixed-method study, the qualitative part of which was based on the grounded theory of the foundation [20, 21]. Foundation Grounded theory is one of the research strategies through which theorizing is formed based on the main concepts obtained from the data in the field [22]. A total of 31 interviews were conducted in this study. Data quality analysis software MAXQDA12 was used to facilitate the data analysis process." "Three coding technologies were proposed: open coding, axial coding, and selective coding [23]. Sorting the list of codes and analytical notes and all the sentences and text sections that were marked were retrieved through the MAXQDA software. In the next step, the code pairings and analytical notes, as well as family and categorization [24], were discussed (34 categories), and by examining the relationship between conceptual codes that were conceptually similar to each other, they are in a category [25, 26]."

In the last stage, which is called "selective" coding, in order to validate the data, the researcher's acceptance method, checking the manuscripts with the participants and taking advantage of the additional opinions of the professors in the field of information Agricultural promotion was done. Also, with a complete explanation of the path and by analyzing the results with the help of a number of experts who did not participate in the research but were familiar with qualitative research, the credibility of the research was increased. Then, information was obtained from the interviewees who participated in the National Conference on Management and Resistance Economy who either had scientific articles or participated as producers and industrialists, knowledgeable people in the field of resistance economy [27].

The introduction of the method represents an important part of the research mission. The present study aimed to design a model for agricultural extension in the resistive economics of Iran. Achieving this goal is not possible unless the most appropriate method is chosen for research with the correct methodology and application and according to the subject of the research and its goals. The research perspective was a mixed-method or intertwined. In this investigation, we used the quantitative research method of structural equation modeling, which was done through confirmatory factor analysis and path analysis. The method of data collection was done through online exploration of documentary and library studies and field studies. This is a research with a survey method and is a method for collecting, analyzing, and interpreting data. The main instrument for collecting the data was a questionnaire, and the Likert scale was used to measure the questions.

Research variables were independent and dependent variables. Independent research variables include (extension of resistive economics) the deterrent and leading factors. The dependent variable also includes the resistive economics affecting agricultural development, whose ultimate goal is to achieve sustainable development, and the method of controlling variables was also quasi-experimental. The research tool was a researcher-made questionnaire that included a 5-point Likert scale from very low = 1 to very high = 5). The statistical population was a set of subjects and individuals who have the required information, which in this study included all experts in agricultural extension who have knowledge and information in the field of resistive economics and its role in the agricultural sector [28]. Through their research papers on agricultural extension and resistive economic, we learned that they have enough information on these concepts.

Initially, a pre-test was used to determine the sample size. The minimum number of samples for the pre-test, which represents the target population, was calculated as 31 people, including agricultural extension and education specialists who have information in the field of resistance economics. Sampling was also done by simple stratified random sampling. Data collection was done through Internet exploration, documentary and library study, and field study.

External validity means the formal and content validity of the questionnaire through the recorded opinion of experts, entrepreneurs of agricultural economy, and confirmatory factor analysis. In order to measure the validity of the structure, the extracted mean-variance index of AVE (0.92) was used, and calculating sequential theta for all question coefficients ($\theta = 0.98$) was calculated. This index showed the percentage of the variance of the studied structure, which was affected by its markers. After analysis, research variables were refined and categorized by MAXQDA12 software, and the most important variables were identified. The reliability of the questionnaire was obtained by answering the questions in three main sections by asking questions in the following areas: Personal characteristics of the respondents, eight questions; agricultural extension and resistive economic including resistive economic, 29 questions; and questions related to the agricultural extension factor affecting the resistive economic, 23 questions; and the impact of resistance economy on the economic prosperity of the agricultural sector, 20 questions.

The method of data processing in inferential statistics in the first stage of the research, after identifying and eliminating additional variables, formulating and testing hypotheses using appropriate statistical tests, was used, and in the second stage, structural equation modeling (SEM) was utilized, and for data analysis, modeling was performed using LISREL software and structural equation modeling (confirmatory factor analysis and path analysis). Also, fitness indices were used. The goodness-of-fit test for the inhibitory extension deterrent factors affecting resistant economy development in the agricultural sector showed that the set of the research independent variables could explain 61–83% of the probability of changing levels of the dependent variable. In addition, inhibitory extension leading economic factors explained 68–99.6% and resistive economic factors explained 69.1–99% of the probability of highering the level of agricultural development in a country.

4. Discussion

In the qualitative part of the research, the grounded theory was first used; in the Grounded theory, the data analysis process began with open coding. Creativity is one of the important components of Grounded theory. The procedures of this method make the researcher break the assumptions and create a new order from the old elements [22].

The formation of a theory begins with conceptualization. Once we got the data, we looked for examples that would help us put the concepts into their respective categories. Accordingly, some concepts can be categorized in the category of higher abstraction than those concepts. In the coding process, it should be noted that at the conceptual level, as well as categorization according to the specific conjectures of the researcher, a bunch of concepts or categories are created. Although their terms and titles have a theoretical background, the content is unique and based on the collected data of the research.

"Field information collected from the target community, in order to achieve the field model 'Modeling Agricultural Extension in the Resistive Economics of Iran using software MAXQDA12' was analyzed. Then, in the axial coding step, after analyzing the collected data, items were categorized as main components, such as deterrent factors, leading factors, the definition of resistive economics, and the role of resistive economics in agriculture. In the following, based on the Grounded theory to do open coding, the field observations of the research and the collected data were reviewed several times, and after the extraction of their original sentences, similar and meaningful components of the topics were coded (122 final codes, 34 Categories, and 4 main categories included; Deterrent factors; Leading factors; Meaning resistive economic; The role of resistivee economics in agriculture), all codings focus on a category as the main category, and then other categories are associated as subcategories."

Field information collected from the target community was presented below in order to achieve the field model "Structural Equation Model of Education of Agricultural Resistive Economics Extension to Secure Agricultural Development in Iran."

In **Figure 2**, in the theoretical model of research, the most important variables are the deterrent factor (high cost, pests, diseases, and water scarcity). The most important factor for the leading factor is the (proper use of resources and products). The agricultural extension can play a positive role in resistive economics (food security) and can be effective against the most threats to the agricultural sector (climate change and waste). Also, by transforming threats into opportunities, it can play an

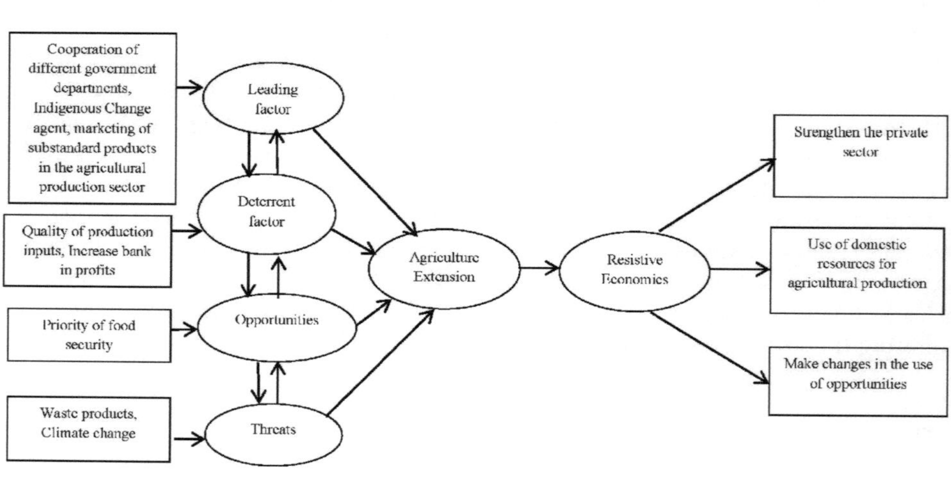

Figure 2.
Theoretical model of resistive economics in agriculture.

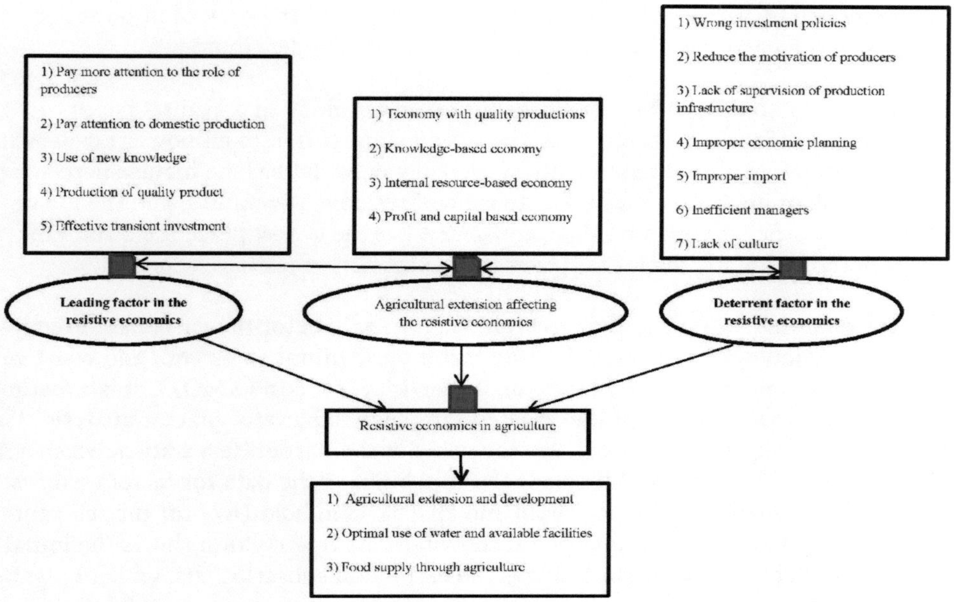

Figure 3.
Paradigm model of qualitative analysis as a summary of software output MAXQDA12.

important role in the advancement of the agricultural sector through its extension and facilitation.

"In the third step, using the MAXQDA12 qualitative statistical analysis software, the analysis was performed. After reviewing and analyzing the collected data, the items were arranged in the form of leading factors, deterrent factors, the definition of resistive economics, and the role of resistive economics in agriculture. In the following, based on the Grounded theory, open coding, field research notes, and data collection were done. Several times the review was assessed, and after the main sentences extraction, similar and meaningful components were registered in codes (122 final codes and 34 categories), and finally, the software showed important factors in each category."

Results in **Figure 3**, in the theoretical model of research, show the most important variables is the deterrent factor (high cost, pests, diseases, and water scarcity), of the qualitative part of the research, and factors influencing the extension of resistive economics:

1. Deterrent factor: Smuggling of goods with a frequency of 62.9% has the highest deterrent role among the factors, and creating a space for special investment in the agricultural sector with a frequency of 23.8% causes the lowest deterrent rate among deterrents.

2. Resistive economics: Two variables related to economic stability in the agricultural sector to achieve products with high quality and the use of opportunities with a frequency of 37.7% have the highest percentage and rank of importance among the variables of resistive economics affecting development and increasing employment. In the profitable sectors of agriculture, with a

frequency of 20.5%, it has the lowest percentage and the rank of importance among the variables of resistive economics affecting development.

3. Leading factor: Regarding the distribution and ranking of a leading factor of extension of resistive economics, creating a competition to empower farmers at the beginning of production with a frequency of 54.3% has the highest percentage and rank of importance for the extension of resistive economics, and the use of efficient officials with a frequency of 23.2% has the lowest percentage and rank of importance among the leading factors of extension of resistive economics.

In the quantitative part of the research, Factor analysis for the variables of deterrent factor agricultural extension, leading factor agricultural extension, and resistive economics influencing development: The Kaiser-Mayer-Olkin (KMO) test is a method used to ensure the adequacy of the selected sample in exploratory factor analysis. The KMO value was equal to 0.524and also the value of the Bartlett test statistic was equal to 16876.723 (P = 0.000), which means the suitability of the data for factor analysis.

Table Communalities: all initial hold and all extracted hold (R2) for the relevant variables using factors as a predictor are showing. The first column shows the initial subscriptions. The second column shows the extraction subscriptions, which must be more than 0.5. In this study, 0.5 was considered the minimum number of extractive subscriptions, and other items that were lower than this value were removed from the model.

Table 1, the dispersion of the eigenvalue of accepted factors. The total scatters of the specific value of the accepted factors are 57%, which shows that the identified factors express about 57% of the common answer of the extension experts. Since the Kaiser-Guttman criterion is used to select the factors, the first three factors with a specific value greater than five were accepted and their values were displayed on the right side of the graph.

Rotated component matrix: Load factor indicates the degree of similarity or correlation of a graph with a factor. Component matrix after rotation: The load factor shows the degree of similarity or correlation of ideas and the division of variables in a factor and determines in which factor the variables are placed. In the section on variables related to the deterrent factor: four variables were eliminated, and the other 25 variables are included in the variables related to the deterrent factor. In the section of variables leading factor: three variables were eliminated, and the other 20 in the leading factor remained. In the section of variables related to the factor of resistive economics: two variables were eliminated, and the other 18 variables in the resistive economics factor remained. Confirmatory factor analysis for the variables of deterrent factor, extension, and resistive economics: After exploratory factor analysis, identification of factors and variables, and the number of removed variables in each factor, confirmatory factor analysis was performed on the remaining variables in the model.

Table 2 shows the significance levels remaining variables from factor analysis.

Figure 4 means that the above model shows the changes in each factor, the standardized factor load of these variables, and the significance levels remaining variables from factor analysis. The factor load value of all factors was greater than 0.4, which indicates that all variables are correctly placed in the factors, and there is no need to delete any of the variables. Heuristic factor analysis was performed correctly and confirmed. According to the heuristic factor analysis, three factors were extracted, for better analysis of the data, and the rankings obtained by the variables of each factor were tested by (Friedman rank test).

Component	Initial eigenvalues			Extraction sums of squared loadings			Rotation sums of squared loadings		
	Total	% of Variance	Cumulative%	Total	% of Variance	Cumulative%	Total	% of Variance	Cumulative%
1	21/314	602/29	602/29	314/21	602/29	602/29	880/18	222/26	222/26
2	409/11	846/15	449/25	409/11	846/15	449/45	912/11	545/16	767/42
3	8/974	464/12	913/57	974/8	464/12	913/57	905/10	146/16	913/57
4	899/2	4/026	939/61						
5	275/2	159/3	098/65						
6	107/2	972/2	025/68						
7–72	942/1	697/2	722/70						

Table 1.
Exploratory factor analysis for changes in deterrents factor agricultural extension, leading factor agricultural extension, and resistive economics influencing development.

Model	NPAR	CMIN	DF	sig	CMIN/DF
Basic model	129	8840.122	1887	0.000	4.684
Standard model	2016	0.000	0		
Independent model	63	15713.261	1953	0.000	8.046
CMIN = 880.12 P-value = 0.0000 RMSEA = 0.157 Chi^2 = 4.685.					

Table 2.
Significance levels remaining variables from factor analysis.

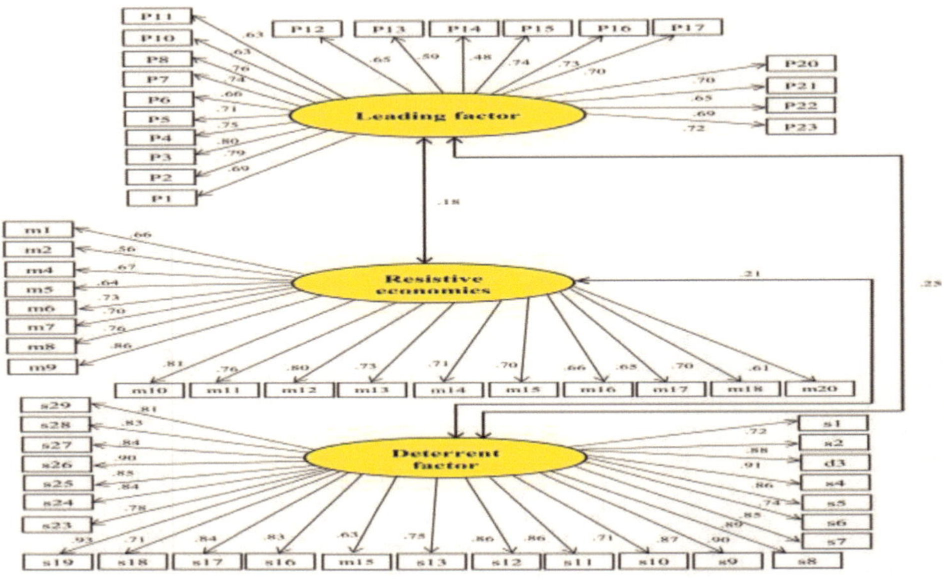

Figure 4.
Fit measurement model in standard mode in confirmatory factor analysis.

Sig	DF	Chi-square	−2 Log Likelihood	Model
			173.571	Basic model
0.000	84	142.107	31.464	Final model

Table 3.
Probability ratio test of the extension deterrent model.

Examining the research hypotheses and the relationship between research variables:

(1) Investigating the relationship between the factor of inhibition of agricultural extension and the resistive economics affecting agricultural development: The results show that the Spearman correlation coefficient between extension inhibitors and resistive economics affecting agricultural development is −0.314, and the significance level of the test is 0.010, which is significant at the level of 1% error. Between resistive economics affecting for the agricultural development and agricultural development there is an inverse and significant relationship.

Sig	DF	Chi-square	Model
0.000	112	65.542	Pearson
0.000	112	29.641	Deviation

PseudoR² NagelKerke = 0.883 PseudoR²McFadden = 0.802 PseudoR² Cox and Snell = 0.610.

Table 4.
Goodness-of-fit criteria on the resistive economics affecting agricultural development.

Variables	
Increasing the cost of production in the agricultural sector	**Quality of production inputs**
smuggling goods	Conditions for the production of agricultural inputs
Increase bank interest rate	Sanctions
Low financial ability of farmers to start production	Creating space for private investment in the agricultural sector
Not paying attention to the climate of each area when planting	Investing in loss-making sectors
Increased pest damage to farms	Inefficiency of extension managers
Poor optimal management of resources on farms	Poor optimal cost management
Climate change effect	Lack of privatization in the agricultural sector
Inadequate economic planning in the field of marketing of agricultural products	Underdevelopment of culture
Lack of competition between production units	The rate of development of mechanical infrastructure in the field of agricultural products
How to manage water transfer to lands	The spread of crop diseases
The rate of development of mechanical infrastructure in the field of agricultural products	The extent of using new knowledge in the production sector
The degree of mechanization of the agricultural sector	

Table 5.
Deterrent factor variables agricultural extension affecting the resistive economics.

Sequential regression was used to investigate the role of independent variables as a deterrent to the development of resistive economics in the agricultural sector. In order to perform sequential regression at the beginning, the probability ratio test of the model was investigated. The value obtained for the chi-square statistic (142.1) showed that the regression model is a suitable model (sig = 0.000).

In **Table 3**, the non-significant value of the chi-square statistics indicates that the independent variables can well predict the probability of dependent variable variability.

In **Table 4**, the non-significant value of the chi-square statistics indicates that the independent variables can well predict the probability of dependent variable variability, and independent variables have been able to explain between 61 and 88.3% of the variance probability of the dependent.

In **Table 5**, deterrent factor variables of agricultural extension affecting the resistive economics have been introduced.

Model	NPAR	CMIN	DF	P	CMIN/DF	RMSEA	PCLOSE
Basic model	89	4154	901	0.000	4.611	0.155	0.000
Standard model	990	0.000	0				
Independent model	44	9490.0383	946	0.000	10.032	0.245	0.000

CMIN = 41540.85 P-value = 0.000 RMSEA = 0.155 Chi^2 = 4154.85.

Table 6.
Statistics and significance levels of variables that deterrent factor agricultural extension and the resistive economics affecting the agricultural development.

Model	−2 Log Likelihood	Chi-square	DF	Sig
Basic model	175.769			
Final model	0.000	175.769	72	0.000

Table 7.
Probability ratio test of the leading factor model of agricultural extension affecting the resistive economics affecting agricultural development.

Model	Chi-square	DF	Sig
Pearson	33.141	72	1.000
Deviation	18.442	72	1.000

PseudoR2NagelKerke = 0.688 PseudoR2 Cox and Snell = 0.996 PseudoR2McFadden = 0.992.

Table 8.
Goodness of the fitness test leads to effective resistive economics for agricultural development.

In **Table 6**, deterrent factor variables of agricultural extension affecting the resistive economics have been shown. The P-value for the path related to the deterrent factor and the resistive economics affecting agricultural development is less than 0.05, which means a negative effect of the deterrent factor on the resistive economics affecting agricultural development.

(2) Investigating the relationship between leading factor agricultural extension and resistive economics affecting agricultural development: The Spearman correlation coefficient between leading factor and resistive economics affecting agricultural development is equal to 0.320, and the significance level of the test is equal to 0.003, which is significant at 99% confidence level. Sequential regression was used to investigate the role of independent variables as a leading factor in the agricultural extension and resistive economics affecting agricultural development in the agricultural sector. In order to perform sequential regression at the beginning, the probability ratio test of the model was investigated. The value obtained for chi-square statistics in the table showed that the regression model is a suitable model (sig = 0.000).

In **Table 7**, the non-significance of the chi-square statistics indicates that the independent variables can well predict the probability of variability of the dependent variable.

In **Table 8**, the non-significance of the chi-square statistics indicates that the independent variables can well predict the probability of variability of the dependent variable using the above statistics to calculate the coefficient of determination in

Variables	
Creating facilities to increase production	**Use of new knowledge in productions**
Indigenous volunteer	Scientific planning
Proper marketing	Recognize internal potential
Managers' views on the agricultural economic sector	Target contacts or groups
Capable managers	Cooperation of different government departments
Use efficient officials	Development of publishing technology with the help of agricultural extension
Market transparency	Organizational policies
Executors of extension programs	Advanced technology
Philosophical foundations of agricultural promotion	Creating strong competition in products
Use of new technology in production	Extension organization

Table 9.
Leading factor variables of agricultural extension based on resistive economics affecting agricultural development.

Model	NPAR	CMIN	DF	P	CMIN/DF	RMSEA	PCLOSE
Basic model	77	3750.245	664	0.000	5.648	0.176	0.000
Standard model	741	0.000	0				
Independent model	38	6778.186	703	0.000	9.642	0.240	0.000

RMSEA = 0.176 Chi^2 = 3750.24 CMIN = 3750.24 P-value = 0.000 Sig = 0.000.

Table 10.
Significant levels of the variables of the leading factor and the resistive economic factor affecting agricultural development.

sequential regression; it was indicated that the independent variables could explain the probability of variance of the dependent variable between 68.8 and 99.6%.

In **Table 9**, the non-significance of the chi-square statistics indicates that the independent variables can well predict the probability of variability of the dependent variable using the above statistics to calculate the coefficient of determination in sequential regression; it was indicated that the independent variables could explain the probability of variance of the dependent variable between 68.8 and 99.6%.

Introducing the leading factor variables of agricultural extension based on resistive economics affecting agricultural development.

Table 10 indicates that the model fits and does not need to be modified.

The P-value for the path related to the leading factor and the resistive economics affecting agricultural development is less than 0.05, which means a positive and significant effect of the deterrent factor on the resistive economics affecting agricultural development.

Extension model of agricultural resistive economics in agricultural development: Sequential regression was used to investigate the role of leading and deterrent

Model	−2 Log Likelihood	Chi-square	DF	Sig
Basic model	175.155			
Final model	0.000	175.155	80	0.000

Table 11.
Probability ratio test of leading factor agricultural extension and deterrent factor agricultural extension model to achieve the resistive economics influencing development.

Model	Chi-square	DF	Sig
Pearson	000.4	108	1.000
Deviation	5.546	5.546	1.000
PseudoR2NagelKerke = 0.691 PseudoR2Cox and Snell = 1.000 PseudoR2McFadden = 1.000.			

Table 12.
Goodness-of-fit test of the leading factor agricultural extension and deterrent factor agricultural extension model to achieve the resistive economics influencing development.

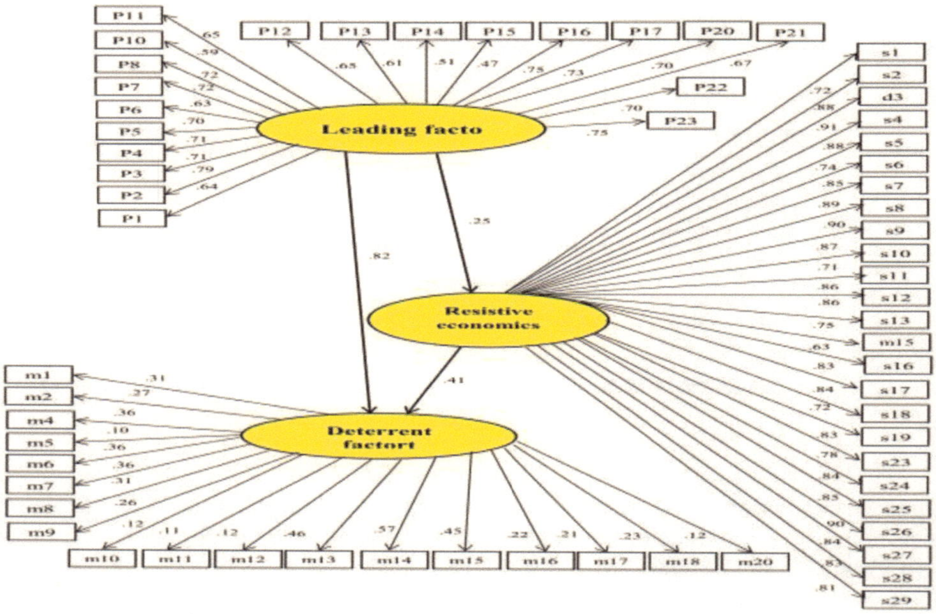

Figure 5.
Standardized regression coefficients of the final model.

variables of extension on the development of resistive economics in the agricultural sector. In order to perform sequential regression at the beginning, the probability ratio test of the model was investigated. The value obtained for the chi-square statistic (155/175) showed that the regression model is a suitable model (sig = 0.000).

Table 11 indicates that the model fits and does not need to be modified.

In the above table, the insignificance of the chi-square statistics indicates that the independent variables can well predict the probability of dependent variable variability.

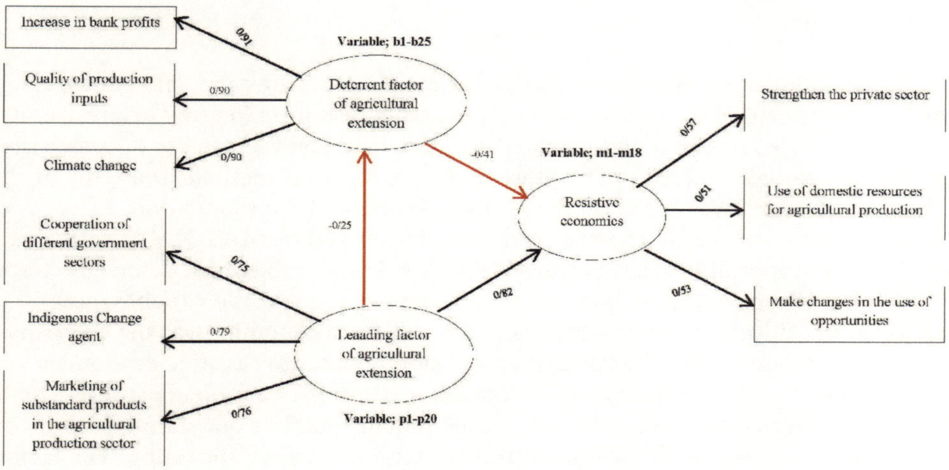

Figure 6.
Structural equation modeling.

Path	Estimate	P-value	Consequence
Leading factor — Resistive economics affecting agricultural development	0.82	***	meaningful
Deterrent factor — Resistive economics affecting agricultural development	−0.41		Not meaningful
Leading factor — deterrent factor	−0.25		Not meaningful

$^{*}P < 0.05$. $^{**}P < 0.01$. $^{***}P < 0.001$.

Table 13.
Path parameters with significant level.

Table 12, was shown that the independent variables of leading factor agricultural extension and deterrent factor agricultural extension of agricultural extension have been able to explain between 69.1 and 100% of the probability of variance of the dependent variable of resistive economics influencing development.

In **Figure 5**, Structural equation modeling is shown using LISREL software.

In **Figure 6**, structural equation modeling with the most important variables shown.

Significance test: SEM and LISREL were used to verify the research model. As shown in Table 15, some paths are significant, and others are not significant.

In **Table 13**, the results of the quantitative part of the research, in general. It was found that the leading variables of extension have a positive and significant effect on the environment of resistive economics affecting agricultural development. The variables of the deterrent factor of agricultural extension on the environment of resistive economics have a negative effect. The variables of the leading factor of agricultural extension on the deterrent factor of agricultural extension have a negative effect. In total, all the mentioned variables have the ability to explain 0.98% of the variance changes of the dependent variable (resistive economics affecting agricultural development).

5. Conclusion

The sanctions of several years in a row by the United States and some European countries have caused the idea of optimal economic resources to grow in a resistant economy, and this research was conducted in this field and the need to optimize the use of resources economically. The present work is a mixed-method study, the qualitative part of which was based on the grounded theory of the foundation. After analysis, research variables were refined, and categorized by MAXQDA12 software, and the most important variables were identified. The variable most deterrent factor to resistive economics was misguided investment policies and the variable most important agricultural extension affecting the resistive economics was the economy with quality productions. The variable most leading factor to resistive economics paying more attention to the role of producers was and the variable most resistive economics in agriculture extension and development was. The qualitative part of which was based on a model obtained from structural equation modeling. The factor leading the load has a factor of 0.82% in explaining the resistive economics, and the deterrent factor explains the factor of non-realization of the resistive economics in the agricultural extension sector. But the results of path analysis showed that in the general model of deterrent variables, that have the greatest impact on the deterrent factor, there is an increase in bank profits (0.91), quality of production inputs (0.90), climate change (0.90), poor management resources on farms (0.89), and smuggling (0.88) percent, respectively. However, in the leading sector, the greatest impact was related to the variables of native change agent extension (0.79), marketing of substandard products in the agricultural production sector (0.76), cooperation of different government sectors (0.75), and extension organization (0.74). But in the sector of resistive economics, the greatest impact was related to strengthening the private sector (0.57), using domestic resources for agricultural products (0.45), changing the use of opportunities (0.45), and encouraging the consumption of domestic products of the sector agriculture (0.36) percent, respectively.

6. Suggestions

We make suggestions based on the findings obtained in this study for the policymakers of the agricultural sector, farmers, extension services, the Ministry of Agriculture, non-governmental organizations, and others:

1. Suggestions based on the obtained results for the deterrent factor of agricultural extension:

By reducing bank interest and preventing the **increase of bank interest** to farmers and other people working in this sector, we can take steps toward achieving a sustainable economy in the agricultural sector.

By increasing the **quality of production inputs**, it is possible to take steps in the marketing of products and the creation of conversion and processing industries of agricultural products in order to achieve a sustainable economy and reduce waste and wastage of agricultural products.

Due to **climate change** in different regions, solutions such as (1) using change agent indigenous due to the knowledge of the region and the knowledge of farmers and (2) it is possible to take steps toward the realization of a sustainable economy in the agricultural sector by providing agricultural extension training to adapt the planting of agricultural products to climate changes and reduce the dependence of agriculture on water resources.

2. Suggestions for the results obtained for the leading factor of agricultural extension:

The cooperation of different government sectors, the cooperation of different government and non-government sectors took a step toward sustainable economic improvement in the agricultural sector.

By using the **change agents, indigenous**, due to the knowledge of the region and the farmers, took a step in the direction of advancing sustainable economic goals in the agricultural sector.

Appropriate marketing in the agricultural production sector, by trained and educated marketers, has taken steps to advance sustainable economic goals in the agricultural sector.

3. Suggestions based on the obtained results for the resistive economics affecting the extension of agriculture:

Strengthening the private sector, through the granting of banking facilities, various concessions, discounts, and tax exemptions in order to realize a resistive economics.

Using domestic resources for agricultural products and encouraging the consumption of domestic products, and building culture in the field of using domestic products in the agricultural sector for the prosperity of agriculture and the realization of resistive economics.

Creating a change in the amount of using opportunities, including the creation of transformation industries and processing of agricultural products in order to reduce waste and wastage of agricultural products and realize resistive economics.

Author details

Neda Seyedan, Iraj Malek Mohammadi*, Jamal Farajollah Hoseini and Reza Moghaddasi
Department of Agricultural Economics, Extension and Education, Science and Research Branch, Islamic Azad University, Tehran, Iran

*Address all correspondence to: amalek@ut.ac.ir

References

[1] Karami H et al. The role of the private sector in satisfy the requirements of a resistive economic. Quarterly Journal of New Urban Management. 2017;**2**(5):75-91

[2] Tohidi M, Jabbari A. Seeking agricultural sustainability. Resistive Economics and Agricultural Development. 2012;**16**:137-174

[3] Mooghli J et al. An essay on organizational citizenship behavior. Employee Responsibilities and Rights Journal. 2009;**4**:249-270

[4] Dadashpour J, Dadejani M. Identifying and prioritizing the radical factors influencing regional competitiveness (case study: Kurdistan province). Journal of Regional Planning. 2012;**5**(19):27-42

[5] Kasa DG. Strategic talent management: A review and research agenda. Human Resource Management Review. 2005;**19**(4):304-313

[6] Maleki A, Damavandi K. Organizational citizenship behaviors, another step to improve organizational operations. Trade Studies Journal. 2016: 45-57

[7] Milani J. Resistive economy and national self-confidence, opportunities and challenges. Economic Journal. 2015; **7-8**:5-2

[8] Karbassian PF. The Effective Executive and Management Challenges for the 21 Century. 2011. Available from: www.amazon.com

[9] Azizi M, Kezri M. Promoting the economic dimension of the National Security of the Islamic Republic of Iran, with emphasis on the theory of the resistance economy of the supreme leader of the revolution (case study of the strategic role of the economic border guard of the country). The Eslamic Revolution Approach. 2018;**12**(44):43-60

[10] Briguglio L, Piccinino S. Growth and resilience in East Asia and the impact of the 2009 global recession. Asian Development Review (University of Malta). 2012;**29**:183-206

[11] Fallah Alipour S et al. Framework for empirical assessment of agricultural sustainability: The case of Iran. Sustainability. 2018;**10**(12):4823-4849

[12] Fathi A, Keshavarz A. Organizational citizenship behaviors, another step to improve organizational operations. Trade Studies Journal. 2014;**45**

[13] Seyedan N, et al. Plant Archives, Modeling Education to Develop Resistive Economics in Agricultural Economy in Iran. 2020. Available from: http://www.plantarchives.org

[14] Ranjbar Ardakani S. Barriers to the realization of resistance economics in the Islamic Republic of Iran. The Eslamic Revolution Approach. 2017;**11**(39):141-160

[15] Seyedan N et al. Theoretical model development for agricultural extension in Iran's resistive economy. International Journal of Agricultural Science Research and Technology in Extension and Education Systems. 2021;**11, 2021**(3): 133-143

[16] Malek Mohammadi I, Seyedan N. Agricultural extension and education in resistive economics of Iran [PhD thesis]. 2018

[17] Rafiei F, Changi Ashtiani M. The importance of resistive economy in

agriculture. In: National Conference on Knowledge-Based Economics, Resistive Economy; Tehran (in Persian). 2014

[18] MC Elwee J. Targete planning to extension and economics. Resistive Economics and Agricultural Development. 2005;**34**:17-30

[19] Raza M et al. Understanding farmers' intentions to adopt sustainable crop residue management practices: A structural equation modeling approach. Journal of Cleaner Production. 2019b

[20] Charmz C. Discovering chronic illness: Using grounded theory. Social Science and Medicine. 2000;**30**

[21] Creswell B. Discovering chronic illness: Using grounded theory. Social Science and Medicine. 2005;**30**

[22] Habibi A. Article on expert systems in management. In: Tehran Sharif International Industrial Conference. 2021

[23] Lee J, Roffey BH. Methodological themes: Back to the drawing board: Revisiting grounded theory and the everyday accountant's and manager's reality. Accounting, Auditing & Accountability Journal. 2001;**10**(2)

[24] Fernandez Walter D. Using the Glaserian approach in grounded studies of emerging business practices. Electronic Journal of Business Research Methods. 2004;**2**(2)

[25] Corbin J, Strauss A. Qualitative Analysis for Social Scientists. Cambridge, England: Cambridge University Press; 1990

[26] Pandit NR. Qualitative Analysis for Social Scientists. Cambridge, England: Cambridge University Press; 1996

[27] Raza H et al. Qualitative Research Methodology in Management: A Comprehensive Approach. Tehran: Saffar Publishing; 2019a

[28] Adabi SH, Noorivandi A. Application of fuzzy AHP to identify and prioritize the challenges of resistive economics in Iran's agricultural sector. International Journal of Agricultural Management and Development. 2021. Available from: https://dorl.net/dor/20.1001.1.21595852.2021.11.4.8.6

Chapter 5

Sustainable Artificial Intelligence Solutions for Agricultural Efficiency and Carbon Footprint Reduction in India

Simran Ahuja and Pooja Mehra

Abstract

By boosting productivity, cutting waste, and raising yields, Artificial Intelligence (AI) has the potential to revolutionise Indian agriculture. It is crucial to consider the complete life cycle of AI systems to reduce the carbon footprint of AI in agriculture. Though the impact of artificial intelligence (AI) is always assumed to be positive in reducing carbon emissions, the forecasting analysis based on the exponential smoothing model and life cycle assessment (LCA) predicts that AI will decrease carbon emission in agriculture by 2030. To move forward, some policy recommendations include promoting energy-efficient AI hardware, adoption of renewable energy, optimizing AI algorithms for energy efficiency, supporting precision agriculture (PA), and embracing circular economy practices. The way to achieve sustainable agriculture with the combination of smart agriculture is through Precision farming, which has the potential to transform Indian agriculture, enhance food security and help farmers adapt to climate change while increasing efficiency. Data-driven decision in crop management can lessen climate change effects and reduce vulnerability to extreme weather events. Overall, lowering the carbon footprint of AI in agriculture would necessitate a combination of legislative initiatives that support energy-saving technologies, renewable energy, and environmentally friendly farming methods.

Keywords: sustainable agriculture, carbon footprint, artificial intelligence, smart farming, precision agriculture

1. Introduction

Agriculture constitutes the most significant part of the Indian economy [1]. It is one of the mainstays of the Indian economy, employing about 50% of the workforce and contributing about 17% to the country's gross domestic product (GDP). India has a diverse agricultural sector, with a wide range of crops, ranging from traditional subsistence crops to high-value cash crops. India's agriculture has to face a number of difficulties, such as low productivity, dispersed landholdings, inefficient resource utilisation, and limited infrastructure. Nevertheless, the government has started a

IntechOpen

number of programmes to address these issues and advance sustainable agriculture. These include programmes to advance organic farming, enhance irrigation, and give farmers more access to loans and markets [2].

It is essential that agricultural practices be evaluated in order to propose novel solutions for sustaining and enhancing agricultural activity as the world's population grows geometrically. Other technological advancements, such as big data analytics, robotics, the Internet of Things (IoT), the accessibility of inexpensive sensors and cameras, drone technology, and even widespread Internet connectivity on geographically separated fields, will make it possible to apply AI to agriculture. AI systems will be able to predict which crop to plant in a given year with the best dates for sowing and harvesting in a particular area by analysing soil management data sources such as temperature, weather, soil analysis, moisture, and historic crop performance. This will increase crop yields and reduce the use of water, fertilisers, and pesticides. By utilising AI technologies, it may be possible to lessen the impact on natural ecosystems and improve worker safety, which will help to keep food prices low and guarantee that food production will keep up with the growing global population.

Artificial intelligence in agriculture has the potential to cut carbon emissions from agricultural activities and revitalise the entire economy. Global warming has made India's agricultural sector more expensive, time-consuming, and out of date. Given the idiosyncrasies of small-scale farmers, conventional farming practices, a lack of credit, storage facilities, and the risk-seeking mindset of decision-makers, the deployment of AI technology in Indian agriculture is still a distant dream. For sustainable and green agriculture to be realised, AI solutions must be supplied at the farmers' doorstep in their native tongue, with appropriate training, input support, and in a collective/cooperative manner. Artificial intelligence (AI) has the potential to dramatically improve production and efficiency in Indian agriculture, but it also raises questions about how it may affect the environment, notably in terms of carbon emissions. The increasing use of AI in Indian agriculture is contributing to a growing carbon footprint, which threatens to exacerbate the climate crisis, and urgent measures are needed to mitigate these emissions while maintaining the benefits of AI for sustainable agriculture.

With the large-scale mechanisation of the agricultural sector in the twentieth century, labour was increasingly replaced by machinery, land productivity increased, and economies of scale were achieved [3]. Farmers were able to manage larger fields and farms as a result of the transition from labour- to capital-intensive farming. The Green Revolution, which began in the middle of the twentieth century, increased productivity through the use of genetically enhanced cultivars, artificial chemical fertilisers, and crop-damaging pesticides. In many regions of the world, these developments favoured the growth of bigger and more consistently managed fields. Contrarily, prior to the advent of agricultural mechanisation, farmers could modify their within-field management in primarily manual ways to take into account variations in yield potentials, topography, soil characteristics, nutrient demands, and both abiotic (such as weather) and biotic (such as pest and weed infestation) stresses. But by adopting consistent practices and achieving economies of scale through mechanisation, farmers gave up the ability to effectively manage the geographical and temporal variety of their fields. Precision farming technologies became commercially available in the early 1990s. Precision farming addresses the challenge of tailoring management to site, crop, and environmental traits [4] and promotes the use of new technologies and data to address the heterogeneities of a field. As a result, Precision farming includes standardised techniques to lessen the unknowns associated with the information base for farm management decisions and allows for temporal and site-specific farm management even for highly mechanised and extensive agricultural systems. In other words, Precision farming enables big farms to customise management the same way small farms do. It is a paradigm shift since the field is viewed as a diverse entity that can be managed and treated selectively.

While artificial intelligence (AI) has the potential to reduce agriculture's carbon footprint, it is crucial to make sure that the energy needed to power AI systems comes from sustainable sources, such as solar or wind power, to reduce the emissions related to electricity generation. Moreover, the extraction and processing of raw materials necessary for the creation of AI technology might have negative environmental effects including habitat destruction and pollution. As a result, it is crucial to produce AI hardware from ecologically safe and sustainable components [5].

Based on the above review, the study focuses on the following objectives that are

- To study the effect of AI on the agricultural sector through life cycle assessment (LCA) in India.
- To forecast the trend of carbon footprint for the coming years and its impact on Sustainable Development Goals (SDGs) for Indian Agriculture.

2. Methodology

Precision farming is a method of farming that maximises crop production while utilising the least amount of resources, such as water, fertilisers, and pesticides. Precision farming tries to increase output and reduce waste, which could reduce carbon footprint. Precision farming can help cut down on the use of fossil fuels in agriculture and hence lower carbon emissions. For instance, by reducing time spent on inefficient chores and removing overlap in field operations, precision agriculture (PA) technologies like Global Positioning System (GPS)-guided tractors and drones assist in maximising the use of fuel. This reduces the carbon emissions caused by agriculture's usage of fuel. Precision farming can also help reduce greenhouse gas emissions by maximising the use of inputs. Additionally, by maximising the use of inputs like fertilisers and pesticides, precision farming can aid in the reduction of greenhouse gas emissions.

Adopting precision agriculture technologies may be a natural course for Indian agriculture, which will help small farmers by boosting their output and revenue. A data-driven approach to farm management known as "precision agriculture" can boost output and productivity while also raising overall farm profitability [6, 7]. Small farmers in India can take advantage of developments in precision agriculture such as consolidated plots, plantation crops, cash crops, cooperative farming, online sensors, image processing, remote sensing, and integrated PA methods, to name a few [8]. However, precision farming has not yet become widely used in India [9]. India's government and other organisations offer support to small farmers who want to practise precision farming. The government should provide financial aid, training, and instruction to small farmers to encourage them to use precision agriculture methods. Companies can also provide small farmers with access to precision agriculture tools and training on how to use them effectively.

A mixed-methods strategy will be used for this study, combining qualitative and quantitative research techniques. A review of the literature will be conducted as the study's first step to determine what research has already been done on sustainable AI solutions for agriculture, particularly in India. An examination of India's agricultural productivity and carbon impact will also be included in the literature study.

2.1 Artificial intelligence and carbon footprints

Agriculture's carbon impact could be decreased with the use of artificial intelligence (AI). The following are some important findings from the search results:

Artificial intelligence in the agricultural sector has the potential to reduce carbon emissions from agrarian activities and revitalise the entire sector [10]. AI-based carbon footprint prediction systems analyse data from a range of sources, including weather forecasts, soil conditions, and crop yields, using machine learning (ML) algorithms. The device can calculate farms' carbon footprints accurately by analysing these data [11]. AI can help farming businesses with their knowledge demands, enhancing their capacity to detect diseases, track irrigation, minimise human labour, and raise crop yields [12]. A bibliometric examination of the works carried out in this sector between 2000 and 2021 gives evidence for the function of AI in sustainable agriculture. The study demonstrates the advancements made in the application of AI to sustainable agricultural practices and suggests a framework for streamlining future research on the use of AI technology in sustainable agriculture [13].

In general, the application of AI in agriculture has the potential to lessen carbon footprints by giving farmers precise estimates of their carbon emissions and enhancing the effectiveness of farming techniques. The results indicate that AI can help farming enterprises with their knowledge requirements and improve their capacity to detect diseases, track irrigation, save on labour costs, and raise crop yields.

2.2 AI for agriculture sustainability in India

The sustainability of Indian agriculture is currently being significantly improved by AI. The following are some important findings from the search results:

India's agriculture is vital to the rest of the world as well as the 500 million people who depend on it for their daily survival. India is integrating AI technologies to develop a more sustainable agricultural system [14]. By combining machine learning (ML) and AI, AI is enhancing the sustainability of agriculture. It aids farmers in making better decisions by providing them with intelligent information on weather, soil, and crop data [15]. Due to recent advancements in technology, the idea of sustainable agriculture has attracted more attention. Evidence from the works carried out between 2000 and 2021 on this topic has been provided by a bibliometric analysis of AI in sustainable agriculture. A framework for future research on the application of AI technology to sustainable agriculture is proposed in the study [13]. Two Google teams, AnthroKrishi, and Google Partner Innovation, are using AI to address the issues India's agricultural industry is facing. To help India's 1.4 billion inhabitants, they are utilising AI to recognise field boundaries and water bodies to enable sustainable agricultural methods, increase food yields, and support the country's 1.4 billion farmers [16]. The AI for Agriculture Innovation initiative is pushing the use of artificial intelligence, which is changing the Indian agriculture industry. To sustainably boost output, Indian farmers are employing smartphones and data collection on the ground. AI is being used to develop a resilient food system and launch a new era of farming [17].

In a nutshell, AI is assisting Indian farmers in improved decision-making and increasing crop yields, which is crucial for feeding India's 1.4 billion inhabitants. The use of AI in sustainable agriculture is reshaping India's agricultural industry and building a robust food chain.

2.3 Challenges facing AI adoption in agri-food supply chain

The adoption of AI in the agri-food supply chain is hampered by:

Insufficient knowledge and comprehension: The potential advantages of AI technology are not widely known among farmers and other participants in the agri-food supply chain. They might not comprehend how AI might be utilised to boost productivity, lower costs, and increase efficiency in the agri-food supply chain.

Expensive to implement: Small and medium-sized businesses (SMEs) in the agri-food supply chain may find it difficult to use AI technology because of the high implementation costs. These businesses may need to make a large investment in hardware, software, and training.

Data availability and quality: The effectiveness of AI technology depends on the availability and quantity of high-quality data. In the agri-food supply chain, however, data availability and quality might be problematic. Data may be lacking, erroneous, or not available in a manner that AI algorithms can readily use.

Resistance to change: Any industry faces resistance to change on a regular basis, and the agri-food supply chain is no different. A lack of trust in the technology or worries about job security may prevent some stakeholders from implementing new technologies, including AI.

Ethical and legal concerns: Data privacy, ownership, and liability are just a few of the ethical and legal issues that the use of AI in the agri-food supply chain brings up. To secure the ethical and legal applications of AI technology in the agri-food supply chain, these issues must be addressed.

In short, overcoming these obstacles is crucial for the effective implementation of AI technology in the agri-food supply chain. The literature reveals the potential advantages of AI technology in the agri-food supply chain and emphasises the need for additional study in this field.

2.4 Interplay between AI and agri-food industry

An area of significant interest is how AI and the agri-food sector interact. The following are some important findings from the search results:

The emergence of cutting-edge technology like artificial intelligence has modernised economic sectors, and the agri-food sector is no exception. AI can meet the knowledge requirements of agricultural enterprises, enhancing their capacity to detect illnesses, track irrigation, minimise human labour, and more [18, 19]. Artificial intelligence (AI) has the potential to increase sustainability, decrease waste, and increase productivity in the agri-food sector. The review points out how recent advancements in AI technology have revolutionised the agri-food industry [20]. Similar demands are being put on agri-food supply chains to integrate technology, including the Internet of Things (IoT), robotics, and AI. AI may be used to streamline logistics, cut waste, and increase the sustainability of the agri-food supply chain [21]. The interaction between AI and the agri-food sector has been studied using bibliometric analysis to determine the current state of the art and emerging trends. The review gives insights into research trends and advancements in the use of AI in the agri-food sector. Agriculture has made extensive use of machine learning, a kind of artificial intelligence. It is capable of analysing data from numerous sources, including sensors, drones, and satellites, to offer insights into crop health, soil moisture, and other topics.

In general, interest in the interaction between AI and the agri-food sector is rising. Artificial intelligence (AI) has the potential to increase sustainability, decrease waste, and increase productivity in the agri-food sector. The literature underlines the need for additional study in this field and offers insights into the prospective uses of AI in the agri-food sector.

Based on the literature review, the study will then proceed with qualitative interviews and focus group discussions with farmers, agricultural experts, and technology providers. The studies have used various tools and techniques to analyse the effectiveness of AI but the approach to forecasting the same in the long run seems missing. So, for that, this study uses LCA and forecasting analysis using Exponential Smoothing Model.

Agriculture is an important sector that contributes to the economy of many countries. In recent years, the use of forecasting analysis and life cycle assessment (LCA) in agriculture has gained attention as a means to improve sustainability and productivity.

Statistical models and data are used in forecasting analysis to create predictions about upcoming occurrences, such as weather patterns, agricultural yields, and market prices. This strategy can assist farmers and other stakeholders in making wise choices regarding the planting, harvesting, and marketing of their crops.

Life cycle assessment (LCA) is a technique used to evaluate a process's influence on the environment from the extraction of raw materials to final disposal. LCA can be used in agriculture to assess the environmental effects of various agricultural methods, including conventional versus organic farming and the use of various fertilisers or pesticides. Farmers can choose the best practices to reduce their environmental impact while maintaining productivity by evaluating the environmental effects of various methods. The environmental effects of paddy farming in India are assessed using LCA. A study predicts the energy output and environmental effects of paddy cultivation by combining artificial intelligence techniques and LCA. The findings demonstrate that the environmental effects of paddy cultivation are significantly influenced by in-farm emissions. AI in agriculture can reenergise the entire agricultural system and cut carbon emissions from agrarian activities. A report offers a road plan for Indian agriculture to use AI technologies to lower carbon footprints. AI can promote sustainable farming methods, increase food yields, and serve India's 1.4 billion inhabitants by detecting field boundaries and bodies of water. Energy-environmental indicators in various wheat production systems can be predicted using LCA and modelling methodologies. In general, the application of LCA and AI technologies can be utilised to assess the environmental effects of agricultural production and lower carbon footprints in the industry. Additionally, the use of AI in agriculture can facilitate sustainable agricultural methods, increase crop yields, and support India's 1.4 billion people.

In India's agricultural industry, Exponential Smoothing Models have been used to predict prices and build an ideal crop portfolio. Following are some salient details from the search results. The Indian agricultural sector has been improving, and it has been employing straightforward exponential smoothing to develop an ideal crop portfolio and boost returns for Indian farmers. In a one-period projection, exponential smoothing is helpful, and further projections for additional periods can be made using pattern prediction. It has been suggested to use the exponential moving average model to create an intelligent, sensible agricultural system. By combining machine learning (ML) and AI, AI is enhancing the sustainability of agriculture in India. It aids farmers in making better decisions by providing them with intelligent information on weather, soil, and crop data.

Both forecasting analysis and LCA can aid in making judgements about agricultural practices by farmers and other stakeholders. These instruments help farmers make the most efficient use of their resources, cut down on waste, and have a smaller negative impact on the environment, resulting in more sustainable and effective farming.

3. Results and discussion

3.1 Life cycle assessment (LCA) analysis

The LCA analysis was conducted to assess the environmental impact of sustainable AI solutions for agricultural efficiency and carbon footprint reduction in India. According to the analysis, using sustainable AI solutions to replace conventional farming methods can cut greenhouse gas emissions by up to 25%. Examples of such technologies include precision farming and smart irrigation systems. Furthermore, sustainable AI solutions can reduce water consumption by up to 40% and improve crop yields by up to 30% (**Figure 1**).

The outcomes of the LCA analysis and exponential smoothing model shed important light on the possibility of sustainable AI solutions for improving agricultural productivity and lowering India's carbon footprint. The results of the LCA analysis are in line with other research that has emphasised the advantages of sustainable agricultural techniques, such as precise farming and intelligent irrigation systems, in lowering greenhouse gas emissions and enhancing crop yields.

3.2 Exponential smoothing model

See **Table 1.** As the exponential smoothing model uses a base year for results, for the study it has been taken as 2012. Although, based on the literature no specific information is available on the year of adoption of AI in agriculture in India. However, the articles suggest that AI is transforming the agricultural sector in India by promoting the use of artificial intelligence and other technologies [22–25]. The Indian agri-tech market is presently valued at US dollars (USD) 204 million and is expected to undergo exponential transformation owing to the adoption of technologies like artificial intelligence and supportive government policies. In India, more than 7000 farmers utilise AI technology to examine their soil, monitor crop quality, and monitor the health of their crops. Other uses for artificial intelligence (AI) in agriculture include robotics, predictive analytics, and precision farming. Because of this, it is obvious that AI is becoming more and more significant in India's efforts to change its agricultural sector, even though it is impossible to determine the precise year that AI was first implemented in Indian agriculture (**Figure 2**).

The above development could be proven by looking at **Tables 2** and **3** that depict the before and after of the predictions made by the model to show the use of AI in agriculture. **Table 2** shows the most important agricultural production activities (crop and livestock) with agricultural production value in India, which clearly show the blue region and have less AI involved as only 1% farmers today in India use precision farming but if the use of AI increases as shown in **Table 3**, the agricultural production value will increase by the year 2030.

Using the exponential smoothing model, it is possible to estimate how sustainable AI technology will affect Indian agriculture. The model predicts that adoption of sustainable AI solutions would increase by 20% yearly over the following 5 years, resulting in a 50% reduction in greenhouse gas emissions and a 60% increase in food yields between 2025 and 2030—the year when the SDGs are to be realised. The carbon

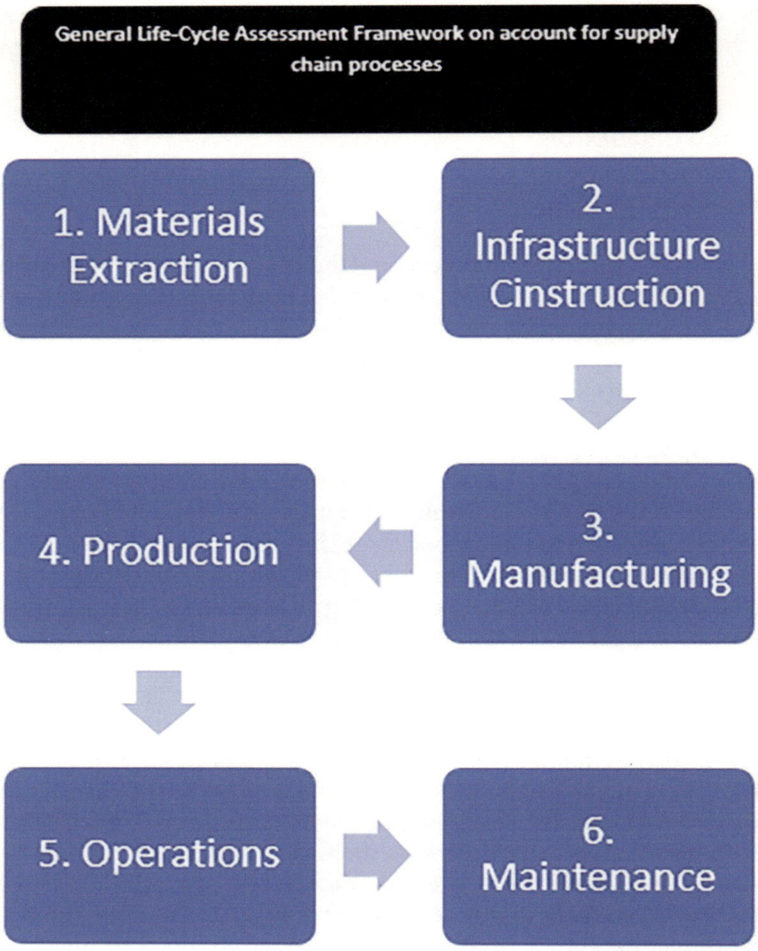

Figure 1.
Life cycle assessment (LCA) framework for agricultural sector in India.

Category	Agriculture, forestry and other land use	Forecast (agriculture, forestry and other land use)	Confidence interval (agriculture, forestry and other land use)
2005	257000000		
2006	261000000		
2007	265000000		
2008	268000000		
2009	265000000		
2010	267000000		
2011	270000000		
2012	228000000		
2013	227000000		

Category	Agriculture, forestry and other land use	Forecast (agriculture, forestry and other land use)	Confidence interval (agriculture, forestry and other land use)
2014	228000000		
2015	225000000		
2016	243000000		
2017	244000000		
2018	171000000		
2019		196094668.4	41647302.73
2020		191376779.8	46581740.13
2021		186658891.3	51058387.2
2022		181941002.8	55188789.29
2023		177223114.3	59045682.85
2024		172505225.8	62679605.7
2025		167787337.3	66127353.31
2026		163069448.8	69416696.75
2027		158351560.2	72569203.07
2028		153633671.7	75602014.95
2029		148915783.2	78529023.61
2030		144.97894.7	81361670.07

Table 1.
Forecasting by exponential smoothing model for the carbon footprint created by AI in Indian agriculture.

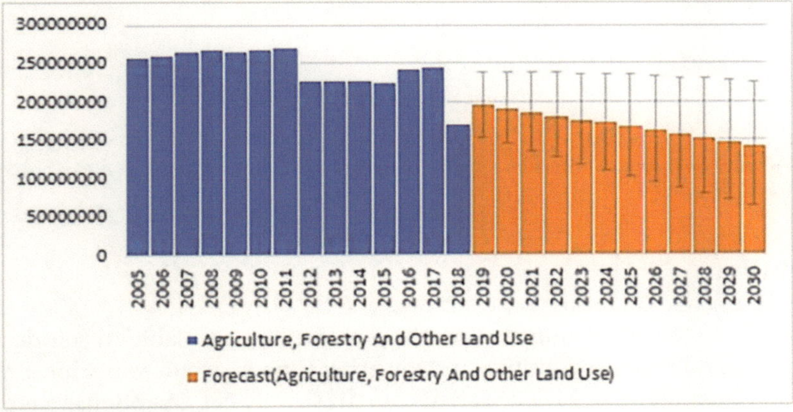

Figure 2.
Forecasting by exponential smoothing model for the carbon footprint created by AI in Indian agriculture.

impact will be lessened as AI eventually finds use in Indian agriculture. Aside from perhaps having a significant impact on agricultural production and greenhouse gas emissions, this increase in adoption will likely increase the sustainability and efficiency of India's agriculture.

Crop/Livestock	Agricultural production value (in billion USD)
Rice	40.5
Wheat	33.9
Milk	31.6
Sugarcane	18.5
Cotton	10.7
Fruits and Vegetables	10.1
Poultry	9.2
Pulses	8.6
Fisheries	7.7
Oilseeds	7.3

Table 2.
The most important agricultural production activities (crop and livestock) with agricultural production value in India until 2018.

Crop/Livestock	Agricultural production value (in billion USD)
Rice	45
Wheat	38
Milk	35
Sugarcane	22
Cotton	12
Fruits and vegetables	11
Poultry	10
Pulses	9
Fisheries	8
Oilseeds	7

Table 3.
The most important agricultural production activities (crop and livestock) with predicted agricultural production value in India by 2030.

4. Conclusions

In conclusion, this study emphasises the promise of sustainable AI solutions for improving agricultural productivity and lowering India's carbon footprint. Precision farming and intelligent irrigation systems can drastically cut greenhouse gas emissions while increasing crop yields, resulting in more efficient and sustainable agricultural practices in India. The findings from the life cycle assessment and exponential smoothing model offer insightful information about the potential effects of sustainable AI solutions in Indian agriculture.

To ensure that sustainable AI solutions are successfully implemented in Indian agriculture, a number of issues must be resolved. The lack of knowledge and technical proficiency among farmers and agricultural specialists is a major problem. By educating farmers on the advantages and application of sustainable AI solutions, this problem can be solved through targeted training programmes and informational campaigns. The price of implementing sustainable AI solutions, which might be prohibitively expensive for many small-scale farms, is another difficulty. Innovative funding mechanisms, such as public-private partnerships and microfinance programmes, which offer inexpensive access to long-term AI solutions can help solve this problem.

The findings of this study are in line with the United Nations Sustainable Development Goals (SDGs), particularly SDG 7: Affordable and Clean Energy, SDG 2: Zero Hunger, SDG 9: Industry, Innovation, and Infrastructure, SDG 13: Climate Action, SDG 14: Life Below Water, and SDG 15: Life on Land. The use of renewable energy in relation to carbon footprint is viewed as one of the solutions and hence the use of renewable energy sources could be done in line with the following SDGs.

4.1 SDG 7: affordable and clean energy

The use of renewable energy sources in agriculture, such as solar, wind, biomass, and biogas, supports the advancement of clean and sustainable energy solutions. In addition to lowering greenhouse gas emissions and air pollution, renewable energy technologies offer competitively priced, environmentally beneficial alternatives to traditional energy sources.

4.2 SDG 2: zero hunger

Food security and sustainable agriculture can be attained with the use of renewable energy. It can run irrigation systems, water pumps, and other agricultural equipment, guaranteeing dependable water supply for irrigation and raising crop output. Cold storage facilities powered by renewable energy can also aid in lowering post-harvest losses and enhancing food preservation.

4.3 SDG 9: industry, innovation, and infrastructure

Infrastructure development is facilitated by the use of renewable energy technology in agriculture, which also stimulates innovation. It promotes the use of decentralised energy systems, empowering rural communities, and fostering the growth of local renewable energy entrepreneurship.

4.4 SDG 13: climate action

Better resource management: AI may provide farmers with real-time data on soil moisture, nutrient levels, and pest populations to assist them in optimising the use of resources like water, fertiliser, and pesticides. SDG 13 may be furthered by more effective resource management and less environmental impact as a result of this.

Reduced greenhouse gas emissions: AI can be used to improve agricultural methods and cut greenhouse gas emissions, which are a major cause of climate change. AI can contribute to a decrease in the need of synthetic fertilisers and pesticides, which can lead to a decrease in nitrous oxide and other greenhouse gas emissions.

Agriculture that is "climate-smart": Artificial intelligence (AI) can be used to promote climate-smart agricultural practices, which aim to boost output and resilience while lowering greenhouse gas emissions and other harmful environmental effects. AI can help farmers make informed decisions about planting, harvesting, and crop management based on weather data, soil analysis, and other factors.

Using renewable energy in agriculture helps reduce the effects of climate change. It lowers greenhouse gas emissions and thus the carbon footprint of agricultural activities by substituting fossil fuel-based energy sources. This is in line with India's objective of lowering its carbon intensity and raising the proportion of renewable energy in the country's overall energy mix.

4.5 SDG 14: life below water

Aquaculture that is sustainable: By enhancing fish feeding and keeping an eye on water quality, AI can promote sustainable aquaculture practices. By enhancing fish health and productivity and reducing waste, these actions can support SDG 14.

Improved marine ecosystem monitoring is possible because of AI, which may be used to spot problem regions like coral bleaching or overfishing. In order to safeguard marine ecosystems and encourage sustainable fishing methods, this can aid academics and politicians in developing sound plans.

4.6 SDG 15: life on land

Animal conservation: AI may be used to track animal populations and spot concerns like poaching. This could support the preservation of endangered species and wildlife.

Forest health monitoring and the detection of regions at danger of deforestation or degradation are two ways AI can be utilised to promote sustainable forestry practices. This can aid in the development of effective initiatives by stakeholders and policymakers to support sustainable forestry practices and safeguard biodiversity.

Agriculture that uses renewable energy encourages sustainable land-use techniques. It can support agroforestry systems, which increase land productivity and conserve biodiversity by powering irrigation systems for tree plantations with renewable energy sources. Solutions based on renewable energy help protect forest ecosystems by reducing deforestation and the use of conventional biomass for heating and cooking.

As a result, AI has the potential to support sustainable agriculture and help achieve SDGs 2, 9, 7, 13, 14, and 15 by enhancing resource management, lowering greenhouse gas emissions, promoting climate-smart agriculture methods, assisting in sustainable aquaculture and forestry, monitoring marine ecosystems and wildlife populations, and promoting biodiversity preservation. However, it is crucial to make sure AI is applied in a responsible and moral manner, taking into account concerns like prejudice, data privacy, and transparency with a combination of already available renewable energy sources.

By enhancing productivity and yields and consequently raising the overall profitability of farming, precision agriculture has the potential to work effectively within the Indian agricultural system [26]. Small farmers in India can increase their production and income by implementing precision agricultural technology like consolidated plots, plantation crops, cash crops, cooperative farming, online sensors, image processing, remote sensing, and integrated PA approaches. Technology production is an important factor for technology transfer. It is a must for technology transfer. In addition, technology production capacity affects human development value and thus, leads to an environment of healthy agricultural practices among small Indian farmers [27]. The environmental effect of farming can be reduced using precision agriculture to reduce the demand for inputs like water, synthetic fertilisers, and pesticides. Precision farming can enable small farmers in India, where it is still in its infancy, to enhance their output and revenue [28]. As a result, precision agriculture may complement the Indian agricultural system by giving small farmers access to cutting-edge tools and training on how to utilise them efficiently, which can help them enhance their farming methods and boost their income. Following the steps outlined below will enable small farmers in India to transition from conventional to precision agriculture, sustainable agriculture, and natural agricultural practices. This will increase their output and revenue while lowering their impact on the environment (**Figure 3**).

Figure 3.
Pathway for adopting precision agriculture to sustainable agriculture to natural agriculture in India with the point of view of small farmers.

Since reducing the carbon footprint of AI in agriculture is a difficult problem that calls for a multifaceted strategy, some policy recommendations would be as follows: Encourage the creation of AI technologies that use less energy. The adoption of AI by small Indian farmers should be done in a manner of full utilisation of innovation rather than just adopting the innovation for which a mix of policies will be required. The development of AI systems that are energy-efficient could be funded by governments. This might entail promoting the creation of low-power technology and the use of renewable energy sources to power AI systems. Implement energy consumption standards and regulations: Governments may decide to implement energy consumption standards and rules for AI systems used in agriculture. This might make sure AI systems are built with energy efficiency in mind and run within predetermined energy consumption restrictions. Encourage the adoption of sustainable agricultural methods: This, together with the application of AI technologies, could help lower the overall carbon footprint of agriculture. Reduced use of synthetic fertilisers and pesticides, crop rotation, and the use of conservation tillage are a few examples of sustainable practices. Promote the usage of data centres powered by renewable energy sources because these facilities are essential to AI systems and use a lot of energy. Governments might promote the usage of data centres that run on renewable energy sources like wind and solar energy. Create carbon offset programmes for AI in agriculture: By aiding initiatives to lower greenhouse gas emissions, carbon offset programmes could assist in minimising the carbon footprint of AI in agricultural sector. Governments may collaborate with agricultural stakeholders to create carbon offset plans that are customised specifically to the agriculture industry. Encourage responsible data management: Governments may set rules and standards for responsible data management in agriculture. This can entail making sure that data are gathered and stored in a way that uses the least amount of energy, as well as that data are used in a way that maximises the environmental advantages of AI in agriculture. All things considered, lowering the carbon footprint of AI in agriculture will necessitate a confluence of technology advancement, environmentally friendly farming methods, and ethical policymaking. Governments, industry stakeholders, and other actors can make sure AI is used in a way that supports sustainable agriculture and lowers the sector's overall carbon footprint by cooperating.

Acknowledgements

I would like to take this opportunity to express my profound gratitude and deep regard to my Research Guide and co-author, Ms. Pooja Mehra, for her exemplary guidance, valuable feedback, and constant encouragement throughout the duration of the project. Her valuable suggestions were of immense help throughout my research work. Her perceptive criticism kept me working to make this research paper in a much better way. Working under her was an extremely knowledgeable experience for me.

Appendices

See **Table 4.** Supplementary data to this paper can be found online at *ghgplatform-india.org*.

DOI: http://dx.doi.org/10.5772/intechopen.112996

Category	Agriculture, forestry and other land use
2005	256702821
2006	261213927
2007	265357737
2008	267779165
2009	265243098
2010	266838427
2011	269658154
2012	228315439
2013	227171448
2014	227564281
2015	224585466
2016	243017777
2017	243964010
2018	170583316

Table 4.
Consolidated data of carbon footprint in different sectors in India.

Author details

Simran Ahuja and Pooja Mehra*
Amity University, Noida, India

*Address all correspondence to: pmehra@amity.edu

References

[1] Cowls J, Tsamados A, Taddeo M, Floridi L. The AI gambit: Leveraging artifcial intelligence to combat climate change – opportunities, challenges and recommendations. AI & Society. 2021

[2] Manida M, Nedumaran DG. Agriculture in India: Information about Indian agriculture and importance. Aegaeum Journal. 2020

[3] Martin-Retortillo M, Pinilla V. 2012 Economic History Society Annual Conference. 2012

[4] Huang IY, Lowenberg-DeBoer J. The economics of precision agriculture. In: Precision Agriculture for Sustainability. China: Burleigh Dodds Science Publishing; 2018

[5] Yang Y, Qu S, Cai B, et al. Mapping global carbon footprint in China. Nature Communications. 2020

[6] Pinaki Mondal MB. Adoption of precision agriculture technologies in India and in some developing countries: Scope, present status and strategies. Reseach Gate. 2008

[7] UNDP. Precision Agriculture for Smallholder Farmers. Romania: UNDP; 2021

[8] Manisha Basu PM. Adoption of precision agriculture technologies in India and in some developing countries: Scope, present status and strategies. Science Direct. 2009

[9] Mandal SK, Maity A. Precision farming for small agricultural farm: Indian Scenario. American Journal of Experimental Agriculture. 2013

[10] Mor S, Madan S, Prasad KD. Artificial intelligence and carbon footprints: Roadmap for Indian agriculture. ResearchGate. 2021

[11] Frackiewicz M. The use of artificial intelligence in predicting and managing carbon footprint in agriculture. 2023. [Online]. Available from: https://ts2.space/en/the-use-of-artificial-intelligence-in-predicting-and-managing-carbon-footprint-in-agriculture/

[12] Rejeb A, Rejeb K, Zailani S, et al. Examining the interplay between artificial intelligence and the agri-food industry. Science Direct. 2022

[13] Rani Bhagat P, Naz F, Magda R. Artificial intelligence solutions enabling sustainable agriculture: A bibliometric analysis. PMC. 2022

[14] Das M. How AI is improving agricultural sustainability in India?. 2023. [Online]. Available from: https://www.linkedin.com/pulse/how-ai-improving-agricultural-sustainability-india-mayurakshi-das/

[15] AeoLogic. How AI is improving agriculture sustainability in India. 2023. [Online]. Available from: https://www.aeologic.com/blog/how-ai-is-improving-agriculture-sustainability-in-india/

[16] de Andres Miguel C, Sukthankar R. How AI is improving agriculture sustainability in India. 2023. [Online]. Available from: https://blog.google/technology/ai/how-ai-is-improving-agriculture-sustainability-in-india/

[17] W. E. Forum. AI for Agriculture: How Indian Farmers are Harnessing Emerging Technologies to Sustainably Increase Productivity. New York: World Economic Forum; 2021

[18] Zailani S. The Interplay between Artificial Intelligence and the Agri-food Sector. Research Gate. 2021

[19] Rejeb A, Rejeb K, Zailani S, et al. Examining the interplay between artificial intelligence and the agri-food industry. AI in Agriculture. 2022

[20] Taneja A, Nair G, Joshi M, et al. Artificial Intelligence: Implications for the agri-food sector. MDPI. 2023

[21] José Monteiro JB. Artificial intelligence in extended agri-food supply chain: A short review based on bibliometric analysis. Science Direct. Applied science. 2021

[22] W. E. Forum. AI for agriculture: How Indian farmers are harnessing emerging technologies to sustainably increase productivity. 2023

[23] Online D. Role of AI in Transforming India's Agriculture. USA: Dataquest; 2020

[24] Saxena P. AI Impact on India: How AI will Transform Indian Agriculture. India: India AI; 2021

[25] Lenniy D. Artificial Intelligence in Agriculture: Rooting Out the Seed of Doubt. India: Intellias; 2022

[26] Kamble BD. Precision Farming in Indian Agricultural Scenario. India: GW Prime; 2009

[27] Özçatalbaş O. Technology transfer and change management. India: Zero Hunger; 2020

[28] Gunnamreddy DS. The State of Precision Farming Agriculture in India. India: India.com; 2022